OAKLAND
A photographic journey
by Bill Caldwell

Looking north from the foot of Broadway

Eight hundred fifty feet above the foot of Broadway looking north

1

OAKLAND

A photographic journey

by Bill Caldwell

Momentum Publications
Oakland, California
Bill@oaklandphotojourney.com
510-653-4311

Find us on the World Wide Web at oaklandphotojourney.com

Editor: *Bill Caldwell*
Photography: *Bill Caldwell, Hasain Rasheed*
Contributing Photography: *Sharon Collier, Phil Bellman, Philip Cohen*
Historic Images: *Oakland History Room, Oakland Public Library, Private Collections*
Writers: *Dennis Evanosky, Betty Marvin*
Contributing writers: *Douglas Duncan, Celia McCarthy, Milan Hájek, David Nicolai*
Cover and Graphic Design: *Milan Hájek*

ISBN 0-9729902-0-8
Printed in Singapore

This book is dedicated to all those who have lived in Oakland,
California over the past 150 years – 1852-2002.

Table of Contents

Momentum Publications would like to thank the Sponsors who helped to make this book a reality.

We would also like to thank the following individuals and companies who purchased books for distribution to the Oakland Unified School District classrooms.

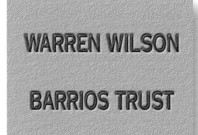

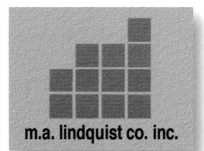

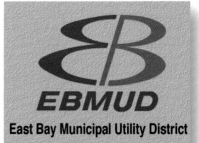

International Association of Firefighters Local 55

Random Acts Firefighters Sport Association

Oakland Black Firefighters Association

INTRODUCTION

**By Senior Oakland City Council Member
Richard Spees
District 4**

Oakland's unique and distinguished history is a story that should be told. In recognition of Oakland's 150th anniversary celebration, Bill Caldwell has created a fitting tribute to our city's rich heritage with his new book, "Oakland - A photographic journey". Through painstaking research, he has collected vintage photographs, sketches, and maps, and contrasted the original images of old Oakland with the matching view from 2002. The result is a moving look back at the city's origin and growth to the "All-America City" of today. What is most exciting about the "Oakland - A photographic journey" project is the opportunity it provides to educate residents and visitors, both young and old, about Oakland's largely unrecognized, but colorful, historical past. I hope that readers join with me in thanking Bill for his efforts to share Oakland's roots.

Dick Spees,
Oakland City Councilmember, 1979-2002

Acknowledgements

Special thanks to:

The History Room of the Oakland Public Library for access to its incredible collection of thousands of historic images of Oakland. And to their always helpful and knowledgeable staff of librarians: Steve Lavoie, Kathleen DiGiovanni and Lynn Cutler.

Milan Hájek for seeing what I couldn't and designing a book that is far better than my original vision.

Annalee Allen for introducing me to Oaklanders who appreciated the importance of this project and for helping with its early development.

Dennis Evanosky for knowing where everything is and for his experience in dealing with the available images of Oakland and for his vast knowledge of Oakland's history.

Husain Rasheed for coming on board as a photographer, becoming a friend on whom I could completely rely to record the images I needed and relieving some of the stress this project placed on my shoulders.

Betty Marvin and Gail Lombardi of the Oakland City Planning Department's Cultural Heritage Survey, for their specialized skills and knowledge, for the ability to magically pull out a complete file on any given subject or location, for eagle eyes spotting problems and mistakes in the text and research and more importantly for knowing how to solve them.

Former Oakland City Councilman Dick Spees for his interest, encouragement and inspiring introduction.

Celia McCarthy for instantly appreciating the value of this project. She was always willing to encourage, share her publishing experience as well as the Port of Oakland's photographic archives, and help in any way she could.

Those financial contributors and advisers who saw the importance of this project and helped make it possible:
Chris Pattillo (the first to come on board) of PGA Design, Greg Chan of East Bay Municipal Utility District, John Dolby of Shorenstein Asset Services, Doug Duncan, David Dunn and Jack Lyness of e-agency, Samee Roberts of the City of Oakland, Darlene Kelly of Prentiss Properties, Mark Lindquist of M. A. Lindquist Co., Sam Nassif of Creative Hospitality Corp., Mannette Belliveau of the Oakland Convention and Visitor Bureau, Diane Castleberry of the Port of Oakland, Frank Barzin and Adrian Perez of Green Copy, Paul Cobb, Gay Caldwell, Conway Jones, Theresa Nelson, Keith Thomas and Warren Wilson.

City officials and employees:
Mayor Jerry Brown, Samee Roberts, Sean O'Shea, Paul Belkin, William Weber, Jim MacIlvaine, Shelly Garza, Cheryl Fabio-Bradford, Joyce Lopes, Police and Firefighters; Sergeant George Phillips, Lieutenant Geoff Hunter, Captain Dave Hector, Lieutenant Howard H. Johnson, Sergeant Doug Wayne, Gary Depp Firefighter – retired, Mike Donner Firefighter.

All those who helped locate or provide photographs: Philip Bellman images of Preservation Park, Carol Brookman of Heinolds' First and Last Chance Saloon, John Chinn of the Oakland Lawn Bowling Club, Philip Cohen, Judyth Collin of the Chabot Space and Science Center, Steve Costa, Steve Lavoie, Kathleen DiGiovanni, Lynn Cutler, Jennifer Dowling, Dennis Evanosky, Tom Flores formerly of the Oakland Raiders, Debbie Gallus of the Oakland Athletics, Debbie Hersh of the Oakland Symphony, Karen Kunzel of the Oakland Ballet, Jeanette Gulledge of the Oakland Zoo, C.J. Hirschfield of Fairy Land, Al Locasale of the Oakland Raiders, Veronica Lee of the African-American Museum and Library, Celia McCarthy of the Port of Oakland, David Nicolai of the Pardee House, Dan Martinez and Julie Baum of the Golden State Warriors, Ray Raineri, Thomas Shunn of the Sequoyah Country Club, Claudia Skapik of the Lakeshore Homes Association. Finally to those who took me to places I could not otherwise gotten to: Robert Cathey, John Law, Thom Hearne and Lieutneant Howard H. Johnson.

Everyone who helped make this book possible in whatever way they could and did.

Lastly, I would like to thank Gay Caldwell for 22 years of support and encouragement.

Preface

During Oakland's past 150 years, tens of thousands of images have been recorded by countless photographers eager to document the city's development. The book you hold in your hands now contains a few of those vintage photos juxtaposed with modern photos shot in 2002 from as close as possible to the same location. This glorious journey makes you feel as if you're entering a time machine: the transition from carriages to cars, from mansions to office buildings and from dirt roads to super highways.

In August, 2001 I was browsing in the Oakland History Room at the main branch of the Oakland Library when a poster caught my eye. It had pictures of all the City Halls of Oakland. It was designed by Eric Kos the previous year for the 148th birthday celebration of the City's founding. That meant that the sesquicentennial would be in 2002. As a photographer and Oakland resident most of my adult life, I began to imagine what it would be like to create a document that looked at 150 years of Oakland's past juxtaposed with the present. I wanted to create a document for Oaklanders today, in 2052 and in 2102. I began searching through photographs, illustrations and books in the Oakland History Room and in private collections. The rich history of Oakland was unfolding through the rare images of the City I was discovering daily. It was exciting to watch the Bay Bridge being built alongside the ferry piers of the late 1800s. There was an old photo of a man on his horse in the middle of a dirt road called Broadway - I imagined the photographer asking the man to keep his horse still for just a bit longer until the necessary long exposure ended. I visualized the laborious 1860s task of preparing a glass plate on the spot and then processing it immediately. My appreciation deepened for the accomplishments of those photographers who came before me. I tapped into this appreciation as I selected images for the book, looking at thousands of images and choosing the ones that moved me, inspired me or contrasted dramatically with what existed in 2002.

I was also inspired by Beth Bagwell's "Oakland, the Story of a City". Her book showed me that a book about a city has tremendous power to change your perspective. It gives you a better understanding of where you live. I could never have imagined some things about Oakland's past that this book contains. I hope that my book will enlighten others as much as Bagwell's did me.

I have created over 60 separate drafts of this book you're looking at. Often I became discouraged, but I knew I could make it a reality, especially with the help and encouragement that seemed to come from everywhere. Goethe said "Whatever you can do, or dream you can, begin it. Boldness has genius, power and magic". That quote hangs on my office wall. These words inspired me to go on; they gave the project the life that the poet promised. I feel fortunate indeed to have had the opportunity to realize my dream.

This book does not attempt to be a definitive visual history of Oakland. It does open the door to examine the places, the rich cultures and individuals that have shaped Oakland's history not included in this volume.

I hope you enjoy this book.

Bill Caldwell
Momentum Publications

Convent of the Sacred Heart   Lake Merritt

The above assembled panoramic image was likely recorded from the bell tower of City Hall in 1879.

In 1879 the downtown district of Oakland was densely populated. The buildings were constructed of wood, and none of the structures survives in 2002.

For the 2002 picture, the objective was to shoot from the same elevation and angle as the old image. The new image was taken from the flag landing (approximately 4th floor) at City Hall looking down on Frank H. Ogawa Plaza with 14th Street on the right.

Photographer likely captured the old panorama from the bell tower.

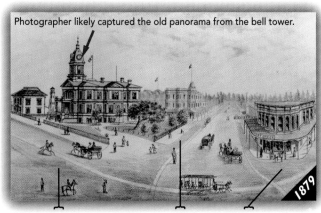

1879

14th Street and San Pablo Avenue at Broadway.

San Pablo Avenue   City Hall Park   14th Street

1879

rly San Pablo Avenue   Frank H. Ogawa Plaza   14th Street

OAKLAND HISTORY TIMELINE

Originally compiled by the Oakland History Room of the Oakland Public Library, this timeline was updated by the Community and Economic Development Agency for the city's 150th anniversary. Usage courtesy of the Oakland History Room of the Oakland Public Library.

1,200 B.C. Ohlone Indians settle in the area that would become Oakland.

1772 Spanish explorers are the first Europeans to visit the East Bay.

1797 Mission de San José is established in what now is Fremont, extending Spanish jurisdiction over the area that would become Oakland.

1820 Don Luis Maria Peralta is awarded a 44,800-acre land grant from the King of Spain that includes most of present-day Alameda County.

1821 The first non-Native American dwelling in what is now Oakland is built by Peralta near Paxton and 34th streets.

1842 Don Luis Maria Peralta divides his land among his four sons. Most of Oakland lies within the shares given to Antonio Maria and Vicente. Logging operations begin in the East Bay Hills by American settlers. At this time California was part of Mexico.

1848 California becomes an American possession with the end of the Mexican-American War.

1849 The California Gold Rush.

1850 California becomes the 31st state in the Union on September 9th. Squatters were ever present on the land owned by the Peraltas.

1851 The first post office is opened in the Oakland House, Oakland's first hotel, at the corner of Broadway and First Street. Mail is addressed to "Contra Costa" (the other coast) until 1855 when the post office recognizes the name Oakland.

1852 On May 4th, the State legislature approves incorporation of the town of Oakland. The hamlet of 70 people was previously known as Contra Costa. The waterfront was granted to Horace Carpentier by town trustees. Immediately, construction of shipping wharves begins along Oakland's Estuary. Building the large wharves and dredging a shipping channel eventually positioned Oakland as an independent point of destination. The Young Ladies' Seminary, predecessor to Mills College, opens in Benicia before moving to Oakland in 1871.

1853 Alameda County is incorporated. The College School (Henry Durant, founder) is established in a rented room on the corner of Fifth and Broadway. It will later become the College of California (1855), predecessor to the University of California. The first public school opens with an attendance of 16. The Oakland Police Department is founded.

1854 The State legislature approves incorporation of Oakland as a city.

1860 Oakland, with a population of 1,543, is ranked 38th in a list of towns of California compiled during the seventh census of the United States. The famed Pony Express makes at least 20 documented rides through Oakland en route from Sacramento to San Francisco, before the transcontinental telegraph system makes it obsolete.

1863 Local railroad service from 7th Street and Broadway runs to the ferry system on the Bay en route to San Francisco.

1864 County supervisors rent an Oakland house to serve as the first county hospital. The first street paving is laid in Oakland, on a small portion of Broadway at a cost of $3.18 per foot.

1865 Mountain View Cemetery, designed by the great landscape architect Fredrick Law Olmsted, designer of New York City's Central Park, is dedicated on May 25th. The first interment is June Weir in July. By 1876, 2,000 burials are recorded. By 2002, there are approximately 165,000 interred there. Many prominent figures in California history have been laid to rest in Mountain View Cemetery.

1867 Dr. Samuel Merritt donates 155 acres around the lake to the city, then dams tidal water from the headwaters of San Antonio Slough. It becomes known as "Merritt's Lake" and later Lake Merritt.

1868 Enoch Pardee builds a home on 11th Street. The family lives there until 1981. Enoch's son George served as Governor of California during the 1906 Earthquake. Carpentier's waterfront lands are transferred to the Oakland Waterfront Company, establishing a railroad monopoly of the waterfront that lasts for four more decades. First Oakland Library Association founded.

1869 The first Oakland horsecar runs from the Estuary to 40th and Telegraph. Oakland becomes the western terminus of the Transcontinental Railroad. The first west-bound train arrives on the Central Pacific railroad in the area now known as Old Oakland. The Oakland Fire Department is established. Antonio Peralta's adobe home in East Oakland is replaced by an Italianate frame house. Still standing in 2002, the house is listed on the National Register of Historic Places and forms the heart of the Peralta Hacienda Historical Park.

1870 The state legislature designates Lake Merritt as a wildlife refuge, the first wildlife refuge declared by any legislative body in North America. By 1870, a Chinese settlement is established in the location of present-day Oakland Chinatown.

1871 Mills College moves to Oakland where a new campus is purchased and Mills Hall is built. In 2002, Mills Hall remains a centerpiece of the college's campus. The City government moves into the newly completed City Hall at 14th & Washington Streets. The Webster Street drawbridge across San Antonio Creek is completed connecting Oakland with Alameda. The city's African American community stands up to the Oakland School Board and fights to preserve open classroom admissions.

1872 The town of Brooklyn is annexed to Oakland.

1874 The first edition of the "Oakland Daily Evening Tribune" is printed. The Federal government dredges the Estuary to open Oakland as a deep water port.

1876 The Camron-Stanford House, an Italianate home, is constructed. Today the last Victorian home to grace the shores of Lake Merritt, the Camron-Stanford House was acquired by the City and becomes the Oakland Public Museum from 1910 to 1967.

1877 City Hall at 14th and Washington Streets burns to the ground in a suspicious fire.

1882 The Oakland Mole (pg. 74) is opened.

1883 Heinolds' First and Last Chance Saloon opens and remains in continuous operation to the present. The bar was a favorite haunt of Jack London who references the bar seventeen times in his novel "John Barleycorn". Heinolds' is designated a National Literary Landmark in 1998 and is listed on the National Register of Historic Places in 2000.

1884 Stick style Cohen-Bray House on 29th Avenue is built as a wedding present to Emma Bray Cohen and her husband Alfred H. Cohen. The home is still owned by their descendants.

1886 Joaquin Miller, distinguished poet, purchases a site in the Oakland hills, naming it "The Hights". Miller plants some 75,000 trees on the 70 acres to create an artists' retreat where the sharing of nature would nurture the creative spirit.

1889 H. C. Capwell opens the Lace House on Washington Street. Several moves later, the H. C. Capwell Company opens the department store at Broadway and 20th Street in 1927.

1891 Oakland's first electric streetcar leaves the foot of Broadway for Berkeley. Residents crowd the sidewalks as if it were a parade. Oakland annexes the Vernon Heights district in what is now known as Adams Point.

1897 Giovanni Ratto opens G. B. Ratto & Company at Sixth and Washington streets and later moves to Ninth and Washington, its current location. The business continues to be operated by family members into the 21st century. North Oakland is annexed to Oakland.

1899 Alexander Dunsmuir builds a spectacular 37-room Neo-classical mansion as a wedding gift for his bride Josephine Wallace. The home, now a museum, offers a glimpse of how the wealthy lived. Today special events are held on its 40-acre estate.

1903 Oakland's first "skyscraper", an 11-story, steel-frame Beaux Arts-style office building at Broadway and 13th Street, houses the Union Savings Bank. Key Route System is established by the Realty Syndicate.

1904 Oakland's first public recreation area, Bushrod Playground in North Oakland, is deeded to the City by Bushrod Washington James.

1906 A major earthquake strikes the Bay Area. San Francisco burns. In Oakland there is scattered damage to many structures but Oakland remains intact. Thousands of San Franciscans flee to Oakland and take up shelter around Lake Merritt. Many people and businesses relocate permanently from fire-ravaged San Francisco.

1907 Frederick Meyer establishes the California College of Arts and Crafts (CCAC) in Berkeley to provide an education for artists and designers that integrates both theory and practice in the arts. In 1923, Meyer purchases a four-acre estate at Broadway and College Avenue and moves CCAC to Oakland.

1909 Oakland adds 44 square miles with the annexation of Claremont, Fruitvale, Melrose, Fitchburg, Elmhurst and other outlying territories. Samuel Merritt College begins as a hospital school of nursing named after Dr. Samuel Merritt.

1910 Oakland's population more than doubles from 66,960 to over 150,000 during the first ten years of the 20th century. Oakland regains control of the long-lost waterfront by final settlement of litigation which had lasted over half a century and cost several million dollars.

1911 Re-incorporation of Oakland under the new city charter adopted in 1910 changes the municipal government from a council to a commission system. U. S. President William H. Taft lays the cornerstone for the new Beaux Arts-style City Hall, said to be the first government building designed as a skyscraper and the tallest building West of the Mississippi when completed in 1914.

1914 The Oakland Civic Auditorium, designed by J.J. Donovan, opens on the shore of Lake Merritt. The auditorium is described as "a California Million Dollar Amusement and Recreation Palace".

1915 The YWCA building at 1515 Webster Street opens, designed by Julia Morgan, an Oakland resident, and the first woman to attend the Ecole des Beaux Arts in Paris. Considered one of her major works, the Oakland Y is the first of eighteen YWCAs designed by Morgan in California and Hawaii.

1918 Over $2 million is spent on construction of factory buildings, an amount not exceeded until 1923. The Edoff Bandstand is built in Lakeside Park.

1921 Mills College confers its first master's degree.

1925 Lake Merritt's "Necklace of Lights" is lit for the first time during the Dons of Peralta Water Festival. There are 126 lampposts, each given by an organization or an individual. The lampposts and 3,400 bulbs shine until 1941 when World War II blackout conditions are enforced. C. L. Dellums helps establish the Brotherhood of Sleeping Car Porters, the first African American trade union in U.S. history. Dellums serves as the union's vice president and president. In 1995, Oakland's new train station is named the C. L. Dellums Amtrak Station.

1926 Charter amendments are adopted which create a permanent Port Commission, and transfer to the County the assessment of city property and the collection of city taxes. Moviegoers flock to the opening of the Grand Lake Theater and are thrilled by the sounds of its mighty Wurlitzer organ.

1927 With the organization of the Board of Port Commissioners, the municipal harbor enters a new era of development as the "Port of Oakland" including the opening of the 700-acre Oakland Municipal Airport. The first successful flight from the mainland to Hawaii leaves from Oakland.

1928 The Fox Oakland Theater opens in downtown Oakland boasting one of the largest stages on the West Coast.

1929 Razing of Idora Park is begun to make way for new homes. For 25 years, the 17-acre amusement park in North Oakland offered a variety of entertainment from roller-coaster thrills to band music and opera. The East Bay Municipal Utility District completes Pardee Dam and the Mokelumne aqueduct delivering fresh water from the Sierra Nevada to Oakland. At 345 feet above the riverbed and 580 feet above sea level, Pardee Dam is the highest in the world at the time

Oakland
May 12, 1852.

The Trustees elect of the Town of Oakland assembled according to previous notice, at 8 o'clock P.M. at the office of Wm Justice Adams.

Present Amédée Marier, A.W. Barrell and Edson Adams, Trustees elect.

Certificates of election were presented by Amédée Marier, A.W. Barrell and Edson Adams, whereupon said Amédée Marier, A.W. Barrell and Edson Adams, having already taken the constitutional oath of office as appears by endorsements upon their certificates of election, took their seats as trustees.

For the purpose of organization Amédée Marier was elected temporary President and A.W. Barrell clerk.

The following Charter was thereupon read and ordered to be spread upon the Journal

An Act to incorporate the Town of Oakland and to provide for the construction of wharves thereat.

The people of the State of California represented in Senate and Assembly do enact as follows:

Section One. The inhabitants of the

Page one of the minutes from the first meeting of town trustees on May 12, 1852. Written by A. W. Burrell, Oakland's first town clerk.

The Oakland Centennial Parade in the summer of 1952
The float is entering Broadway from 14th Street heading north.

The Oakland Centennial Parade in the summer of 1952
Inscribed on the float: "The U. S. Navy salutes Oakland on its Centennial, Oakland Naval Supply Center."

The 150th Anniversary Celebrations May 3rd and 4th, 2002
On May 3, 2002 in Frank H. Ogawa Plaza city, state and national politicians saluted Oakland on its 150th birthday.

Mayor Jerry Brown

California State Senator Don Perata
Councilmember Richard Spees, District 4
Councilmember Danny Wan, District 2

Barbara Lee,
U.S. House of Representatives Member,
District 9

During the anniversary celebrations Saturday May 4, the city honored nationally known artists from film, television, theater, music and dance with a "Key to Creativity." Honorees included Mark Curry (Master of Ceremonies), Ted Lange, Tom Hanks, Mark Hamill, Lenny Williams, Pete Escovedo, Sheila E, Kente Scott, En Vogue, members of Tower of Power and many other artists who have called Oakland "home".

Oakland native Mark Curry, actor, comedian,
Mayor Jerry Brown and Mark Hamill
Mark Hamill accepts an Oakland Creativity Award.
He is best known as Luke Skywalker in the
first three Star Wars films.

Oakland's favorite Pete Escovedo
entertains the crowd
at Frank H. Ogawa Plaza

Mark Curry and Michael Morgan
Oakland native Michael Morgan, right,
conductor of the Oakland East Bay Symphony,
accepts an Oakland Creativity Award.

1930 Adoption of charter amendments provides for a city manager-council form of government.

1931 The Paramount Theatre, designed by Timothy Pflueger in the Art Deco style, is one of the last movie palace extravaganzas to be built in the Great Depression era.

1932 The WPA-built Oakland Municipal Rose Garden blooms for the first time. Some 6,000 rose bushes bloom between May and September.

1934 Voters approve the East Bay Regional Park District which grows from 10,000 acres of former watershed lands in the East Bay hills to 50,000 acres in Alameda County and 42,000 in Contra Costa County including 59 regional parks and recreation areas, 29 inter-park trails, 10 freshwater swimming areas, two golf courses, and 18 children's play areas.

1935 Construction of the new Moderne-style Alameda County Courthouse on the shore of Lake Merritt, one of the Depression-era WPA construction projects that helps stimulate employment.

1936 The Oakland-San Francisco Bay Bridge, one of the engineering wonders of the world, opens months before the Golden Gate Bridge.

1937 The Broadway low-level tunnel connects Oakland with Contra Costa County. Amelia Earhart begins her ill-fated around-the-world flight from the Oakland Municipal Airport.

1941 The Port of Oakland voluntarily turns over to the Armed Forces such facilities needed for the war program. In the ensuing years, the port area becomes the site for the Oakland Army Base and the Naval Supply Center. Filling tidelands for these bases is spectacular. A hill is literally moved to the sea when thousands of yards of soil are hauled around-the-clock in heavy diesel trucks at the rate of one per minute. Dedicated as a memorial to California poets and writers, the WPA-built Woodminster Amphitheater and Cascades open in Joaquin Miller Park.

1942 The Permanente Foundation Hospital is dedicated in Oakland to serve Kaiser shipyard workers. It becomes the first in the chain of Henry J. Kaiser's health plan hospitals.

1943 The Pacific Coast leads the nation in shipbuilding. Oakland leads the West Coast with over 35% of the entire Pacific Coast cargo ship output. Food packing is another major industry with 60% of food stuffs coming from Oakland canneries. Oakland is truly an "arsenal of democracy".

1944 Dr. Bebe Patten establishes the Oakland Bible Institute which is later re-named Patten College to reflect the institution's growth and expansion of academic programs and degree offerings. The Mai Tai, a refreshing rum cocktail, is created at Trader Vic's restaurant.

1945 The day after V-E day, Oakland residents vote more than $15 million in bonds for city improvements including swimming pools, new playgrounds, police, court, streets and sewers, a central library and four new branch libraries.

1946 In the Oakland General Strike, 100,000 union workers walk off jobs throughout the East Bay, to protest anti-union practices of local employers and politicians.

1948 The last Oakland streetcar, Grove Street No. 5, rolls into the car barn. Motor buses replace the trolleys.

1950 Children's Fairyland opens in Lakeside Park. The U.S. Census puts Oakland's population at 384,575, swelled by huge numbers of workers who flocked to the city for WWII jobs. Oakland's African-American population soars from 8,462 in 1940 to 47,562.

1951 From one playground in 1904, the City's recreation areas now number 112 including swimming pools, community centers, baseball diamonds and general playgrounds. The new main library opens at 14th and Oak streets.

1952 Oakland celebrates its centennial with a variety of pageants, programs and exhibits.

1953 The Oakland Board of Education organizes the Oakland Junior College and develops Merritt Junior College.

1959 The Morcom Amphitheater, located in the Oakland Municipal Rose Garden, is dedicated. The amphitheater becomes a favorite location for weddings.

1960 Construction begins on the airport's new jet runway. The Oakland Raiders start playing in the new American Football League.

1961 The first container ships begin arriving in Oakland marking the beginning of dramatic growth of cargo tonnage handled through the Port of Oakland. Fukuoka, Japan, becomes Oakland's first sister city.

1964 Construction of Bay Area Rapid Transit system (BART) begins. The Port constructs the Seventh Street Marine Terminal, the largest single container terminal on the West Coast. Oakland Junior College is renamed the Peralta Community College District.

1966 Bobby Seale and Huey Newton organize the Black Panther Party for Self-Defense at Merritt College. The $25.5 million Oakland-Alameda County Coliseum complex opens near I-880.

1968 Major League Baseball comes to Oakland when Charles Finley moves his Kansas City Athletics into the Oakland-Alameda County Coliseum. They become the Oakland Athletics.

1969 Construction on City Center begins with funding provided from matching grants tied to BART construction. The Oakland Museum of California opens and is one of the most architecturally interesting museums in the country. Comprehensive permanent exhibits on three floors portray nature, history and art: California's natural wonders; events, eras and people who have shaped the state; and the art that Californians produced.

1971 The San Francisco Warriors of the National Basketball Association leave San Francisco's Cow Palace, for the new Oakland-Alameda County Coliseum Arena and become known as the Golden State Warriors.

1972 BART begins operation with its control center above the Lake Merritt station. The Oakland Athletics win their first World Series.

1973 The Paramount Theatre reopens in its original Art Deco splendor following a full and authentic restoration. The authenticity of the renovation is even more remarkable given it was accomplished with a $1 million budget. The Paramount pioneered the reuse of movie palaces for the performing arts. Marcus Foster, Oakland's first black school superintendent, is assassinated by the Symbionese Liberation Army. The Oakland A's win the World Series for a second time.

1974 BART's transbay tube opens for operation. Oakland designates the Western Pacific Depot on Third and Washington Streets as its first city landmark. The Athletics make it three straight World Championship victories.

1975 Nakhodka, Russia, and Sekondi Takoradi, Ghana, become Oakland's second and third sister cities. The Golden State Warriors take the NBA Championship in a four-game sweep over the Washington Bullets.

1977 Lionel Wilson is elected the first African American mayor of Oakland. The Oakland Raiders win their first NFL championship before a record Super Bowl crowd plus 81 million television viewers, the largest audience ever to watch a sporting event. Super Bowl XI's final score: Oakland - 32, Minnesota - 14. The Oakland Tours Program begins offering free walking tours for school groups and interested visitors.

1981 The Oakland Raiders are victorious (27-10) over Philadelphia in Super Bowl XV.

1982 Oakland enters into its fourth sister city agreement with the Chinese city of Dalian. The Oakland Raiders move to Los Angeles.

1983 The Oakland Tribune becomes the first major metropolitan newspaper owned by an African-American when Robert C. Maynard acquires the paper.

1984 Following a $15 million refurbishment, the Oakland Civic Auditorium is reopened as the Henry J. Kaiser Convention Center.

1986 Ocho Rios, Jamaica, joins Oakland's roster of sister cities.

1987 Oakland welcomes Livorno, Italy, as its sixth sister city.

1989 The 7.1 Loma Prieta earthquake hits the Bay Area collapsing the Cypress Freeway and destroying over 1,000 housing units in Oakland. Forty-five people perish. City Hall suffers structural damage and is evacuated. The earthquake-delayed World Series concludes with an Oakland A's victory over the San Francisco Giants.

1991 A catastrophic wildfire rages through the Oakland-Berkeley Hills destroying over 2,500 dwellings in Oakland and Berkeley. Twenty-five people perish. Preservation Park opens, first conceived in the mid-1970s . This unique urban redevelopment project contains 16 Victorian homes (five original to the site, 11 assembled from other locations) converted to offices for nonprofit organizations. The homes are set in an urban park landscaped to resemble a typical 19th century residential Oakland neighborhood.

1993 The National Civic League designates Oakland as an "All-America City". National Oceanic and Atmospheric Administration and Rand McNally rank Oakland's climate the best in the U.S. The Oakland A's Rickey Henderson steals his 1066th base and becomes the all-time leader in stolen bases.

1994 Oakland adopts Historic Preservation Element of General Plan.

1995 Oakland City Hall reopens following an $80 million seismic retrofit and renovation. Fortune ranks California's "Golden Triangle" - Oakland, San Francisco and San Jose - as the #1 place to do business in the U.S. After 13 years in Los Angeles the Raiders return to Oakland. The Potomac opens for dockside tours and Bay cruises following a 12-year, $5 million restoration. The 165-foot-long vessel served as President Franklin D. Roosevelt's beloved "Floating White House" from 1936 until his death in 1945.

1997 In honor of the 60th anniversary of Amelia Earhart's attempt to circumnavigate the world, Linda Finch successfully completes the around-the-world flight, beginning and ending her flight at Oakland Airport's historic North Field. An extensive $121 million renovation to the Oakland-Alameda County Arena adds 72 luxury suites and 3,900 club seats and increases seating capacity for basketball games to 19,200.

1998 City Hall Plaza re-opens after a $124 million rebuilding. Named in honor of late Oakland City Councilmember Frank H. Ogawa. Ogawa was the first Japanese-American to serve on a City Council in the continental United States. Money magazine ranks Oakland among the top 25 cities to live in the U.S. and the 10th best in the West. The final phase of the Cypress Replacement portion of the Nimitz Freeway is completed at a cost of $1.2 billion nine years after the Loma Prieta earthquake collapsed the previous structure. The Downtown Historic District, encompassing 58 structures and 6 city blocks, is listed on the National Register of Historic Places in recognition of its historical and architectural significance.

1999 Jerry Brown, former Governor of California and three-time Presidential candidate, is inaugurated as Oakland's 47th mayor. By the late 1990s, over 130 structures have been declared city landmarks and six areas have been named preservation districts.

2000 The U.S. Census counts 399,484 residents in Oakland and ranks Oakland residents eighth in the U.S. in overall educational achievement. More than one-third of Oakland's residents have a college degree, twice the national average. American Association of Electronics ranks Oakland third in the nation for percentage of households with Internet access. The Wall Street Journal ranks Oakland the Number 1 office market in the U.S. through 2005. The Cuban city of Santiago de Cuba is officially recognized as Oakland's seventh sister city.

2001 Listed on the National Register of Historic Places, the Rotunda Building reopens following a $43 million renovation. The Beaux Arts masterpiece has a 125-foot atrium dome. Forbes magazine ranks Oakland the 10th best city for business in the U.S. Based on U.S. Census Bureau data, the Center for Women's Business Research ranks Oakland third in the U.S. in the number of women-owned businesses. Bill Caldwell begins research and photography on this book.

2002 Oakland celebrates its 150th anniversary. State of California estimates put Oakland's population at over 400,000. The African American Museum and Library, a division of the Oakland Public Library, opens following an $11.2 million renovation and seismic retrofit of the Charles Greene building (c. 1902). The Port of Oakland celebrates its 75th anniversary. Jerry Brown is elected to a second four-year term as mayor of Oakland.

Native peoples of the Bay Area
Ohlone men display talent for expression.
The missionaries forced them to wear the loincloths.

Traditional Native Dancers May 4th, 2002
(Oakland's 150 anniversary celebration):
Musicians – Douglas and Dasan Duncan, Lanny Pinola, Clayton Duncan;
Dancers – Mayabax Duncan, Ruben Ramos, Travis Duncan

The indigenous people of the Bay Area, particularly Oakland, date back thousands of years. Some of the bands in the area were known as the Muwekma, Chochenyo and Tamien. These were only a few of the Ohlone bands in the area. Their villages were located on the upper creek areas, such as Trestle Glen, in the redwood hills near Holy Names College and on the Temescal Creek near the intersection of Claremont and Telegraph avenues. They navigated the waters of the bay and creeks for fishing and travel to neighboring villages. There are still many undiscovered villages within Oakland. The area was abundant with all of their needs. Staying in balance with nature and respecting her is why they survived. The many tribes shared an abundance of fish, elk, birds and small game. They learned to gather strawberries, blackberries, acorns, tules and other roots to both eat and utilize in their daily lives. They gave thanks to *Wa-haad-de-ka* (God-Creator) through ceremonial prayer, songs and dances for letting them live in what has been now known through time as the Garden of Eden.

In the past before any influences from the outside world, the people developed a society that showed respect to all that existed around them. Within the tribe the elders (men and women) carried the knowledge and wisdom, the councilmen delivered to the people through a meeting what shall be done for the tribe. The younger men and women carried out the daily duties for survival of the tribe. The people prayed and danced to the spirits. This is a survival instinct of all people, fear of death. Our people gambled to pass the time, not to gain status, but today the feeling is different. The people want to gain monetarily, to try to escape their oppression within a conquering society. Environment, drugs, alcohol, peer pressure, respect and a lack of understanding of our people, are only a few other concerns that we face. The native children of today are confused and searching for identity. The teachings from our elders today are to respect all that exists and oneself, to keep the culture alive, but learn all you can to survive in today's society. With this one will gain respect for self and from society.

... Contributed by Douglas Duncan

The Bay Area native peoples were hunters and gatherers, living harmoniously with the natural environment for thousands of years.

Members of the Pomo, Yuki, Kato and Maidu tribes, Nate' Peake, Ledah, Douglas and Dalina Duncan.

Vicente Peralta
(1812-1871)

The Peraltas were the first non-indigenous family to settle in the East Bay. In 1820, California's last Spanish governor, Don Pablo Vicente de Sol, granted Sergeant Luís María Peralta 44,800 acres in recognition of his forty years of military service. Luís himself never lived on the land he named Rancho San Antonio. His four sons lived here, caring for the family's livestock and raising their families. Luís' son Antonio lived in the original family home. Vicente, Domingo and Ignacio built their own homes in other parts of the grant. In 1842, an aging Luís María Peralta divided the rancho among his four sons. Antonio received 16,067 acres of land from 68th Avenue to present-day Lake Merritt and up the eastern side of Lake Merritt to Indian Gulch, now known as Trestle Glen. Antonio's portion also included the peninsula of Alameda. Ignacio received approximately 9,416 acres from southeastern San Leandro Creek to approximately 68th Avenue in Oakland. Vicente received the acreage that included the entire original town of Oakland, from Lake Merritt to the present Temescal district. Domingo received all of what is now Albany and Berkeley and a small portion of northern Oakland. Only two houses remain: Ignacio Peralta's 1860 brick house as part of the Alta Mira Club in San Leandro and the 1870 Victorian-era frame house Antonio built, now the centerpiece of Peralta Hacienda Historical Park in Oakland's Fruitvale district.

Vicente Peralta's home in North Oakland
Near the Temescal Creek off Telegraph Avenue near 55th Street.

**Site of the homestead
of Vicente Peralta today**
Corner of 55th Street and Telegraph Avenue in North Oakland. A plaque in front of the Chevron station honors Vicente Peralta. The Peralta house likely would have been located on the left at Vicente and 55th streets.

Antonio Peralta's Home
In 1870 Antonio replaced the family adobe home which was destroyed in the 1868 earthquake with an Italianate-style house.

**Peralta Hacienda
Historical Park**
*2465–34th Avenue.
The house is presently a museum, an Oakland City Landmark and is listed on the National Register of Historic Places.*

17

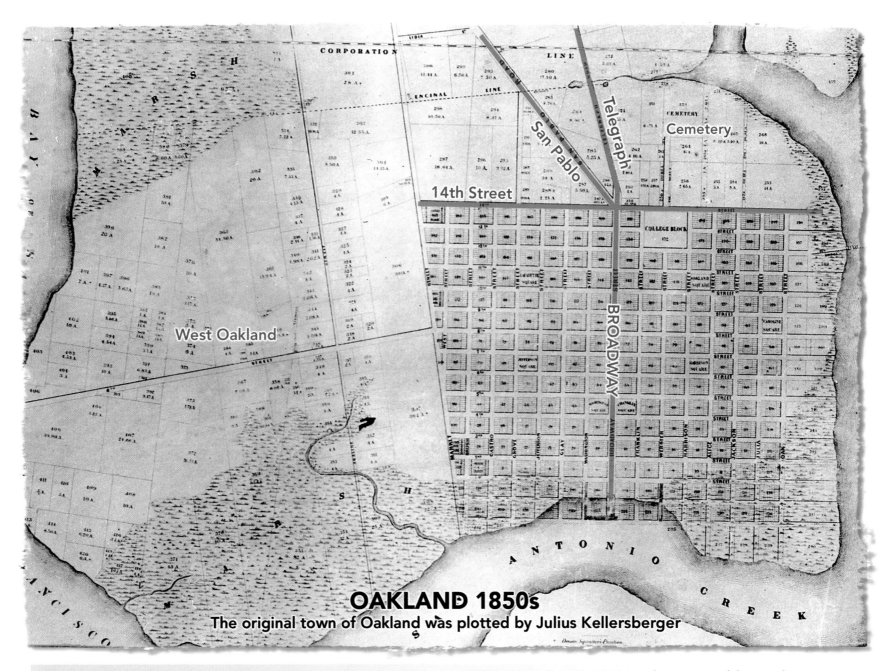

OAKLAND 1850s
The original town of Oakland was plotted by Julius Kellersberger

- May 4, 1852 – Oakland was incorporated as a town.
- 1850s – The journey west from New York could be completed by sailing around Cape Horn, an arduous 4-month voyage, or by sailing to the Isthmus of Panama, then crossing the jungle to the Pacific Ocean and sailing up the west coast of North America, or over land by train to Saint Joseph, Missouri, and from there travel by wagon train, enduring five months of severe misery to the Pacific coast.
- 1852 – Population of Oakland was 70.
- 1852 – One man controlled the waterfront: Horace Carpentier, one of the founders of Oakland.
- 1853 – First public school opened at Fourth and Clay streets.

- 1853 – Henry Durant's private academy accepted three students. Durant's California College eventually became the University of California.
- 1853 – Three newspapers began publishing: the Alameda County Express, the Contra Costa, and the Oakland Herald.
- 1854 – Oakland was incorporated as a city.
- 1857 – Oakland's second cemetery was located out of town – present day location between Franklin and Harrison from 17th to 18th streets.
- 1860 – Population of Oakland was 1,543.

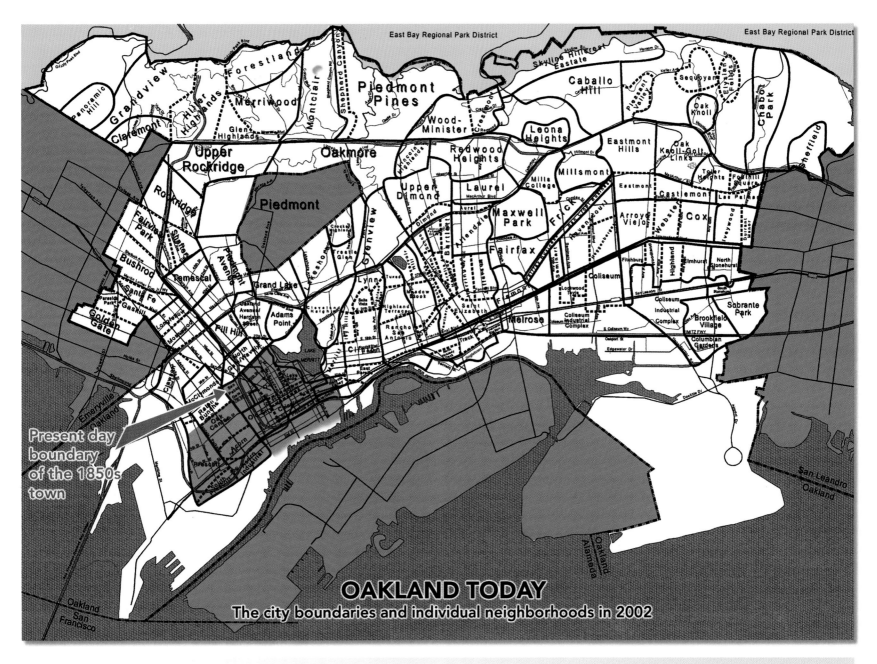

OAKLAND TODAY
The city boundaries and individual neighborhoods in 2002

Present day boundary of the 1850s town

- 2002 – Oakland encompasses 56 square miles of land, with 19 miles of coastline to the west and magnificent rolling hills to the east.
- 2002 – Population of Oakland estimated at 400,000.
- 2002 – Oakland is an international gateway with more than $24 billion worth of goods passing through the Port of Oakland each year.
- 2002 – Oakland is ranked the nation's 8th best city for business in the Forbes annual survey of Best Places in America for Business and Careers, as part of the fifth largest regional economy in the United States with a Gross Regional Product exceeding $300 billion.
- 2002 – Oakland's stunning bay views, parklands, open space, great weather and proximity to the Pacific Ocean make it one of the most beautiful urban areas in the nation.
- 2002 – Total number of businesses is approximately 26,000.

- 2002 – Downtown Oakland has a daytime workforce of more than 76,000.
- 2002 – Oakland is at the heart of the East Bay Regional Park District, a splendid system of 59 parks and 29 regional hiking trails covering more than 92,000 acres in Alameda and Contra Costa counties.
- 2002 – Oakland is the western terminus of the Union Pacific Railroad lines which connect to most major national rail destinations.
- 2002 – The Port of Oakland adds two new marine terminals, with 12 new Super-Panamax cranes, and a new Joint Intermodal Terminal (JIT).
- 2002 – More than 200 flights a day on 13 domestic and international airlines to 34 nonstop destinations pass through Oakland International Airport.
- 2002 – Money magazine ranks Oakland as the 6th most popular city to live in the U.S.

Looking south on Broadway at Sixth Street

This photograph must have been tough to record because images were still being shot with long exposures on glass plates.

Today, a bicyclist replaces the horseman, the Nimitz Freeway passes overhead.

Looking north on Broadway from 12th Street

Workers in foreground are likely laying gas lines for businesses along Broadway. The population grew with the arrival of the transcontinental railroad and demand for goods and services rose dramatically. The west coast terminus was located at the foot of 7th Street in 1869. The population was over 10,000.

Early 20th century Beaux Arts skyscrapers on the eastern side of Broadway from 11th to 17th streets.

First Unitarian Church
At the corner of 14th and Castro streets. Dedicated in 1891, it became an East Bay cultural center.
Designed by Architect Walter J. Matthews. Isadora Duncan danced her debut and Jack London married here.
Now designated as City, State and National Historic Landmark. In the background stands the Ronald V. Dellums Federal Building.

**Broadway at
San Pablo Avenue**
*(see pages 26 and 27
for more images in this series)*

The illustrations on the following pages were created for a Directory of Oakland businesses in 1896.
To be listed and have the business highlighted in the directory, one had to pay a fee to the publishers.

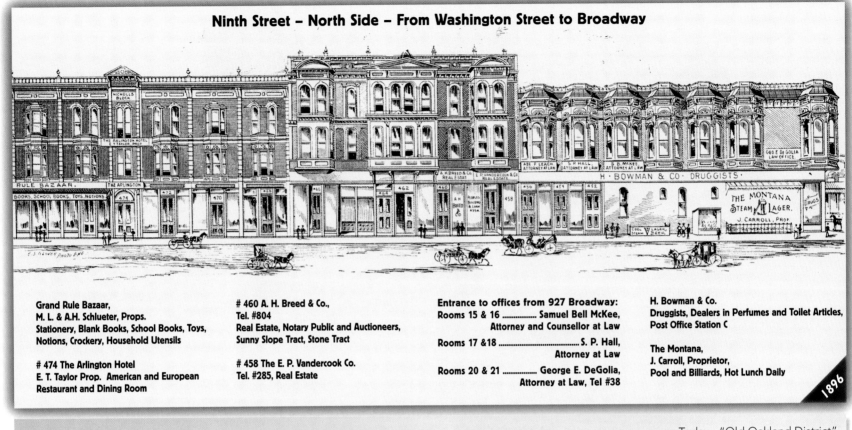

Ninth Street – North Side – From Washington Street to Broadway

Grand Rule Bazaar,
M. L. & A.H. Schlueter, Props.
Stationery, Blank Books, School Books, Toys,
Notions, Crockery, Household Utensils

 # 474 The Arlington Hotel
E. T. Taylor Prop. American and European
Restaurant and Dining Room

 # 460 A. H. Breed & Co.,
Tel. #804
Real Estate, Notary Public and Auctioneers,
Sunny Slope Tract, Stone Tract

 # 458 The E. P. Vandercook Co.
Tel. #285, Real Estate

Entrance to offices from 927 Broadway:
Rooms 15 & 16 .... Samuel Bell McKee,
Attorney and Counsellor at Law
Rooms 17 &18 .... S. P. Hall,
Attorney at Law
Rooms 20 & 21 .... George E. DeGolia,
Attorney at Law, Tel #38

H. Bowman & Co.
Druggists, Dealers in Perfumes and Toilet Articles,
Post Office Station C

The Montana,
J. Carroll, Proprietor,
Pool and Billiards, Hot Lunch Daily

1896

Today - "Old Oakland District"
was extensively restored
in the1980s.

#494 PSAI Old Oakland Association
Old Oakland Property Management

#472 ApotheCom Association

#460 California Health Care Foundation

Smart and Final
Bulk Groceries; entrance on Broadway

The second and third floors of this block are offices.

22

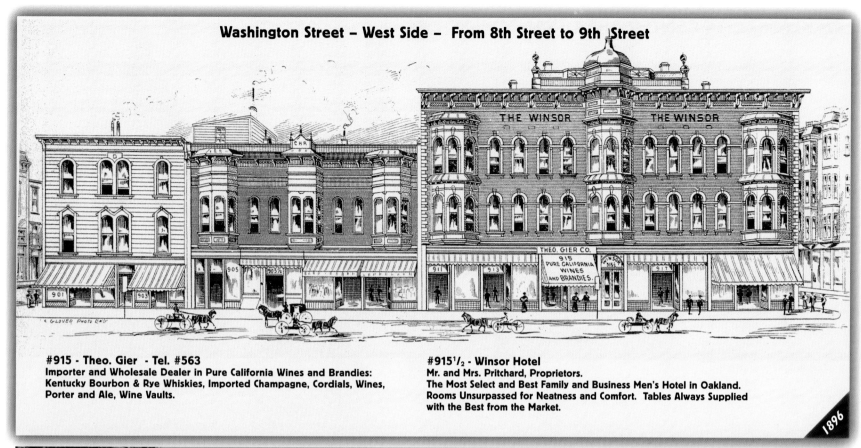

Washington Street – West Side – From 8th Street to 9th Street

#915 - Theo. Gier - Tel. #563
Importer and Wholesale Dealer in Pure California Wines and Brandies: Kentucky Bourbon & Rye Whiskies, Imported Champagne, Cordials, Wines, Porter and Ale, Wine Vaults.

#915½ - Winsor Hotel
Mr. and Mrs. Pritchard, Proprietors.
The Most Select and Best Family and Business Men's Hotel in Oakland. Rooms Unsurpassed for Neatness and Comfort. Tables Always Supplied with the Best from the Market.

1896

This block is part of a designated Historic District. The Ratto Building is a City Landmark.

#801 Schiller's Fine Foods
 # 807 Old Oakland Hotel

#807 Flowers / Travel
#811 Legogo

 # 817 Caffe 817
 # 821 G. B. Ratto & Co.
International grocers

 # 825 Ratto Block *Offices*
 # 827 The Rex

23

OAKLAND CITY CENTER AREA TRANFORMATION

The map below shows the original blocks of downtown before redevelopment. (Also see the highlighted area in picture on page 30)

The map below shows the City Center Complex. Washington and 13th streets are interrupted. (For aerial image, see page 31)

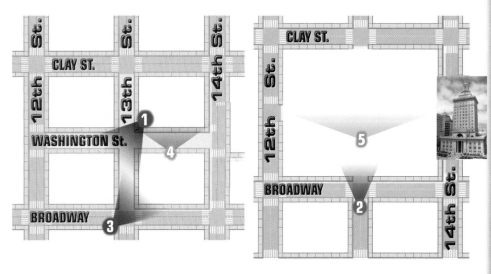

Southeast corner of 13th and Washington streets

Northwest corner of 13th Street and Broadway

13th Street at Broadway
Looking west into City Center with John B. Williams Plaza in the foreground. The entrance to the 12th street BART station is directly below; the Ronald V. Dellums Federal Building is in the background.

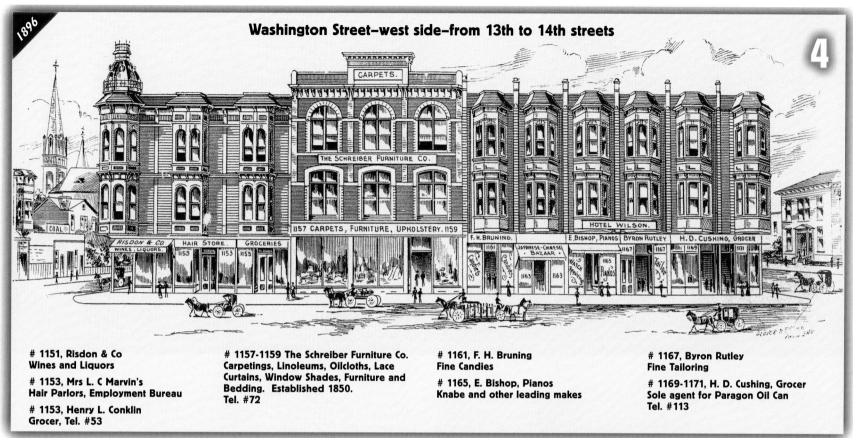

Washington Street—west side—from 13th to 14th streets

1896

4

1151, Risdon & Co
Wines and Liquors

1153, Mrs L. C Marvin's
Hair Parlors, Employment Bureau

1153, Henry L. Conklin
Grocer, Tel. #53

1157-1159 The Schreiber Furniture Co.
Carpetings, Linoleums, Oilcloths, Lace
Curtains, Window Shades, Furniture and
Bedding. Established 1850.
Tel. #72

1161, F. H. Bruning
Fine Candies

1165, E. Bishop, Pianos
Knabe and other leading makes

1167, Byron Rutley
Fine Tailoring

1169-1171, H. D. Cushing, Grocer
Sole agent for Paragon Oil Can
Tel. #113

5

City Center (Looking west at the former corner of 13th and Washington streets)

City Center has 31 shops, 18 restaurants plus tens of thousands of square feet of office space.

25

Oakland's First City Hall
stood on Broadway between 3rd and 4th streets.

Shattuck Hall at 8th Street and Broadway
This building served as the second City Hall from 1867 to 1871

Third City Hall erected in 1871

Oakland's first permanent city hall at 14th and Washington streets. A suspicious fire destroyed the building in 1877.

The Fourth and Fifth

Oakland's fifth City Hall soared above the fourth City Hall, which stood from 1877 to 1914. The fifth City Hall was the tallest building west of Chicago when completed in 1914. It cost $1,893,688 to build.

City Hall
on Washington at 14th streets
The Jack London Oak stands in the center of the park. The entrance to City Hall faced Washington Street.

Looking East
from the 16th floor
of City Hall toward Broadway, with the Tribune Building on the far right and City Hall Park in the foreground.

City Hall Today
Main entrance opens onto Frank H. Ogawa Plaza. Seismic retrofitting and renovation costs to the building after the 1989 earthquake were approximately $80 million, it reopened in 1995.

City Hall Park is now Frank H. Ogawa Plaza.

27

The changing face of the intersection of
14th Street - San Pablo Avenue - Broadway

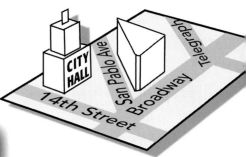

14th Street and San Pablo Avenue at Broadway

This intersection was home to George Lee's garden until his untimely death in 1857. George C. Potter bought the property from the Lee family for $11,000. The photograph depicts Potter's Garden with a grove of oak trees in 1869.

(Also see page 21 for another picture of this intersection.)

Oakland boomed after the arrival of the transcontinental railroad in 1869. By the 1890s Oakland was an extremely important West Coast city and a desirable place to live. Notice electric street car on the right, telegraph wires and all around activity compared to the serenity of the top image.

Victorian-era wooden structures gave way to 20th-century architecture in the downtown area. The First National Bank's skyscraper opened in 1909 with a bank at street level and seven stories of offices. In later years it would become known as the Broadway Building.

The Broadway Building underwent major retrofitting after the 1989 earthquake. An addition was constructed, and the entire complex was rededicated as the Lionel J. Wilson Building, 150 Frank H. Ogawa Plaza. Today the building is part of the city of Oakland's administration complex.

Wilson was the first African-American mayor of Oakland. Ogawa was the first Japanese-American to be appointed to a city council seat of a major metropolitan city in the continental United States.

Note the "Cathedral Building" on the right in the background at Broadway and Telegraph Avenue. This Gothic Revival skyscraper was built in 1913 is designated a City Landmark. Below ground BART trains transport thousands of commuters daily.

Telegraph Avenue

Broadway

San Pablo Avenue

Kahn's Department Store

City Hall

Tribune Tower

Athens Athletic Club

Masonic Temple

Downtown shopping district replaced by City Center in the 1970's

1930

ABOVE OAKLAND

Kaiser Center

Lake Merritt and Lakeside Park Looking East in 1964

1964

Highway 24

Interstate 580

Interstate 980
connector

Elihu M. Harris
State Building

Ronald V. Dellums
Federal Building

555 City Center

Convention Center

Old Oakland
Victorian Row

Ordway
Building

Broadway

City Hall

Tribune Tower

EBMUD
headquarters

**Lake Merritt
and Lakeside Park
today.**

Lakeside
Park

Kaiser
Center

Ordway
Building

ABOVE
OAKLAND

The residence of the William H. Raymond family
1109 Clay Street between 11th and 12th streets.
Mr. Raymond was co-owner of Raymond & Ely Mining Company.

c.1879

555 City Center
12th and Clay streets. Operated by Shorenstein Asset Realty, it opened in 2002.

12th Street and Broadway

c.1871

Athens Athletic Club
On Clay between 12th and 13th streets. Club operated from 1925 to 1968.
The building was demolished in 1977.

Ronald V. Dellums Federal Building
On Clay Street between 12th and 14th streets.

Elihu M. Harris State Office Building
On Clay Street between 14th and 16th streets.

Taft and Pennoyer Building
Department store on Clay Street between 14th and 15th streets.

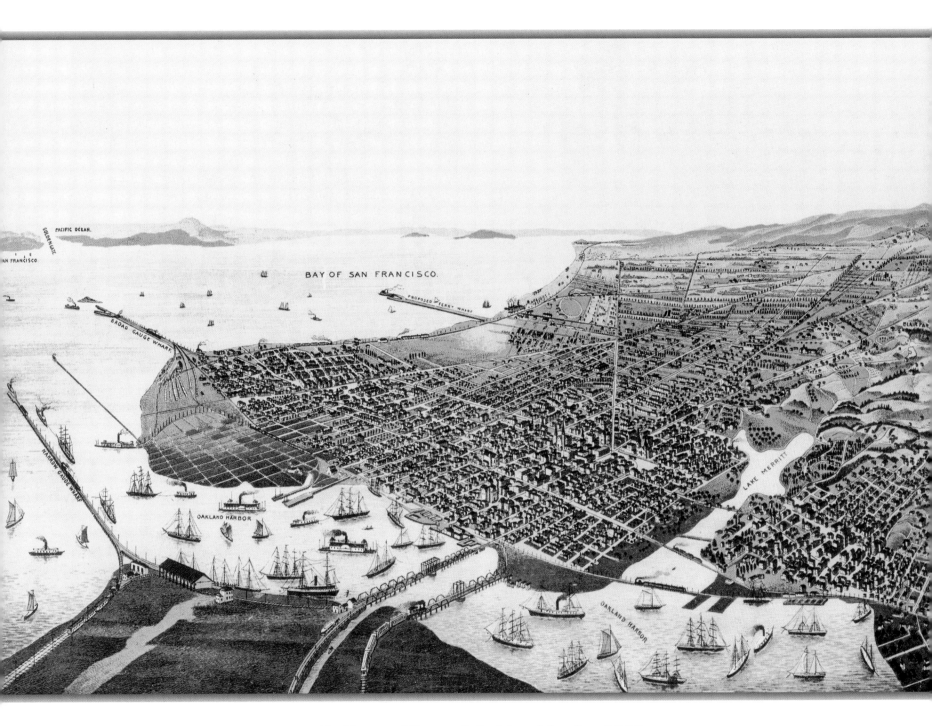

Bird's-eye View of Oakland in the 1880s

This view of Oakland in the 1880s shows the important role that the Oakland Estuary, referred to here as Oakland Harbor, played in the everyday life of both Oakland and Alameda. Ferries, schooners and merchant ships crowd the waterfront. Bridges at Webster and Alice streets span the Oakland Harbor. Other bridges bring trains from East Oakland into downtown. Trains, ferries and merchant ships worked together to facilitate commerce at the turn of the 19th century.

Interstate 880
Nimitz Freeway

Ronald V. Dellums
Federal Building

Loft district

Tribune
Tower

Soccer Field at
Estuary Park

Jack London
Aquatic Center

Kaiser
Center

Alameda County
Court House

Laney
College

Henry
J. Kaiser
Events Center

Lake
Merritt

Lake
Merritt
Channel

5th Avenue
Marina

c.1894

American President Lines (APL) Terminal
The APL complex at the Port of Oakland opened in 1969 and expanded in 1974. It includes the site of the former Moore Dry Dock, a shipyard that operated in Oakland from 1909 to 1961.

Oakland's Estuary
The Estuary was famous as a sheltering winter harbor in the late 19th century. It later became a graveyard for the decaying hulks of square-riggers.

c.1950

Break-bulk operations at the Port
Conventional cargo gear for older general cargo ships was the yard-and-stay rig, with shipboard booms to transfer cargo between the dock and the ship. Fork lifts and pallets, introduced in the 1930s, increased break-bulk efficiency.

Hanjin Terminal
This facility, the first of two container terminals to be completed under the Port's Vision 2000 expansion program is served by four super post-Panamax ship-to-shore gantry cranes. Each has the capacity to lift over sixty metric tons with a sixty-five meter outreach, making them capable of working vessels up to twenty-two containers wide.

c.1918

Municipal Dock 1 between Grove and Clay streets

Navy vessels are moored near the transit shed and smoke pours from PG&E power stacks. This site was later the Grove Street Terminal, and was reconfigured in 1982 as the Charles P. Howard Terminal, the easternmost of the Port's container terminals.

Charles P. Howard Terminal

The terminal is located between Martin Luther King Jr. Way (formerly Grove Street) and Clay Street. This facility combined break-bulk and container operations until 1995, when the wharf and yard were enlarged and reconfigured solely for container use.

Municipal Dock 1

A steamship is docked at the quay wall next to the transit shed. Longshoremen stack and move crates by hand, the traditional method of break-bulk cargo movement. The coal bunkers at Howard Terminal can be seen the distance. This site was redeveloped as the Grove Street Pier, which opened in 1928.

APL Terminal

Looking southeast toward the former Alameda Naval Air Station and the Todd Shipyard. Regionally, the Port of Oakland generates nearly $7 billion in annual economic impact and supports 44,000 jobs.

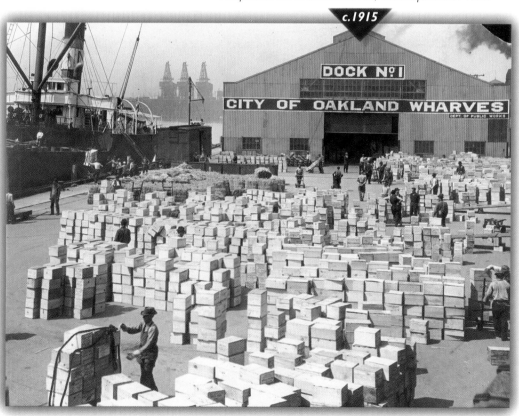

c.1915

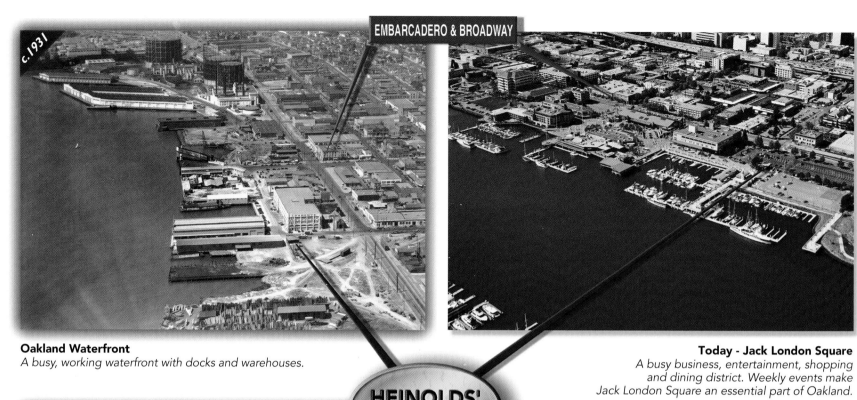

EMBARCADERO & BROADWAY

Oakland Waterfront
A busy, working waterfront with docks and warehouses.

HEINOLDS'
FIRST AND LAST CHANCE

Today - Jack London Square
A busy business, entertainment, shopping and dining district. Weekly events make Jack London Square an essential part of Oakland.

George Heinold, son of Johnny Heinold, is sweeping up - that part of the job didn't change for today's bartender Jim Aunan.

Broadway Pier
*The ferryboat Garden City docked at the foot of Broadway.
This boat traveled the Estuary to San Francisco.*

Jack London Square
*Portfest in 2002 celebrating the 75th anniversary
of the Port of Oakland.*

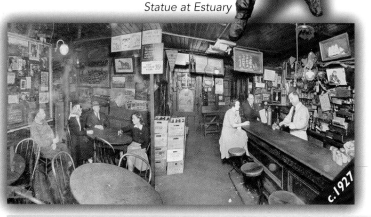

Jack London and Johnny Heinold

*Jack London's
Statue at Estuary*

Heinolds' First and Last Chance Saloon

*Johnny Heinold opened the saloon in 1883 as J.M. Heinolds' Saloon. This historic landmark looked much then as it does today. It was built in 1880 from the timbers of an old whaling ship over the water in a dock area at the foot of Webster Street. For nearly three years, the building was used as a bunk house by the men working the nearby oyster beds. Johnny purchased the building for $100, and with the aid of a ship's carpenter transformed it into a saloon where seafaring and waterfront men could feel at ease. During the 1920s, the ferry that ran between Alameda and Oakland stopped next to the saloon, making it truly a commuter's **First and Last Chance** for refreshments. As the years wore on, many servicemen left for overseas from the Port of Oakland, and the **First and Last** tradition stuck, so the name of the saloon was officially changed to Heinolds' **First and Last Chance.***

***Interior of the Saloon then and now.** Designated a National Literary Landmark, City Landmark, and is listed on the National Register of Historic Places.*

c.1903

G. B. Ratto and Company
The grocery store at 6th and Washington streets opened in 1897. Pictured are: Giovanni Ratto with an unidentified associate.

G. B. Ratto International Groceries
827 Washington Street between 8th and 9th streets. Pictured are store manager Elena Durante Voiron, (great granddaughter of the founder Giovanni Ratto) and staff.

Olander's Saloon

*East 12th Street and 13th Avenue.
Pictured from left to right are:
A. Olander, bartender,
Jack London, first American author
to earn $1 million with his craft,
and an unidentified captain
of Oakland's Police Department.*

*The saloon was built in the 1880s
at the center of the town
formerly known as Brooklyn,
adjacent to LaRue's Landing
where ferries departed
for San Francisco.*

Jack London Club

*1247 East 12th Street at 13th Avenue.
Pictured from left to right are:
Kurt Norton, bartender
(film director, private eye),
"Jack London" George Rowan, Jr.
(real estate broker, musician, tennis professional),
Ralph M. Lacer, Oakland Police captain.
Olander's is now the 2,000-square-foot
Jack London Club, used
for film productions and
very special parties.*

c.1860

Oakland's first hotel
This hotel is likely the Contra Costa Exchange or the Lovegrove House, both located near the Embarcadero, 1st Street and Broadway.

Grand Central Hotel
12th and Harrison streets
Built in 1873, destroyed by fire in 1880.

c.1880

c.1911

Claremont Hotel *on a postcard, now* **Claremont Resort and Spa.** *Designated a City Landmark in 2002.*

Waterfront Plaza Hotel
10 Washington Street on the Estuary. Originally known as the Boatel; one could dock a boat and stay overnight.

The Oakland Marriott City Center
10th Street and Broadway

c.1927

Lake Merritt Hotel
*1800 Madison at Lakeshore
Originally opened as the
Madison–Lake Apartments
in 1927.*

*Today, it is dwarfed by
the brand new Essex
luxury apartment
complex on the left.*

Lake Merritt

The Convent of the Sacred Heart was established in 1868 as a Catholic boarding school for young ladies on the lake's western shore.
In 1957 the campus moved to Mountain Blvd. The name was later changed to Holy Names College. The Kaiser Center now occupies its former location.

WILD GAME REFUGE, LAKESIDE PARK, OAKLAND, CALIFORNIA

Lakeside Park, Lake Merritt
First national wildlife sanctuary in America. Bellevue Staten apartments in the background is on the National Register of Historic Places.

Convent of the Sacred Heart

Facing the western shore when Lake Merritt was crowded with single family estates.

Camron-Stanford
House

Old Lake Merritt
Boat House

Scottish Rite Center

The Essex   Kaiser Center

Lake Merritt is a saltwater lake with an adjoining 122-acre park, a short distance from downtown. The Camron-Stanford House at 14th Street is now the sole survivor of the 19th century era mansions that once lined the western shore of the lake.

Rock • Ridge • Place
Broadway at Rock Ridge Boulevard in North Oakland.
The pillars at the entrance of the development are under construction.
North Oakland's population rapidly increased during the early 1900s.

Rockridge
Broadway and Rock Ridge Boulevard in North Oakland.

Montclair
Likely looking from LaSalle Avenue toward Mountain Boulevard. The Montclair district has its origin in "Fernwood," home of John Coffee Hays,
Texas Ranger and first elected sheriff of San Francisco. Wide-spread automobile ownership made residential development possible beginning in the
1920s. The Sacramento Northern railroad line ran behind Montclair village. Present image - looking from LaSalle Avenue toward Mountain Boulevard.

13th Avenue, the end of the line
*The road we know now as 13th Avenue served as
a logging road for the redwood lumber harvested from the hills.
The lumber trade was among the first to flourish on the Estuary.*

13th Avenue
*The Estuary shoreline today is about three quarters of a mile
from where it once was. Landfill from the development
of the railroads reshaped the area.*

East 14th Street at Fruitvale Avenue
*The rural village of Fruit Vale derived its name from its orchards
that spawned a thriving canning industry. It became a part
of Oakland in 1909 and is now known as Fruitvale.
The flags likely designate a holiday.*

International Boulevard at Fruitvale Avenue
*East 14th Street was renamed International Boulevard
for the diverse population and businesses in the area.*

Idora Park

A major amusement park from 1902 to 1928. Located in the Temescal District of North Oakland, from Telegraph to Shattuck avenues between 56th and 58th streets. Today Idora Park tract, developed in the 1930s, is distinguished by period revival houses, distinctive streetlights and underground utilities.

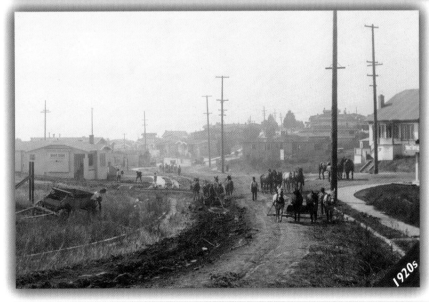

Maxwell Park

In the 1920s this land of ranches, farms and dairies became a residential neighborhood. Average price of a newly built home was under $6,000. Today a quiet, hilly neighborhood in central East Oakland, from High Street to 55th Avenue between MacArthur Boulevard and Brookdale Avenue.

MacArthur Boulevard at Piedmont Avenue

Moss Avenue at Piedmont Avenue
Moss was among the many Oakland streets renamed MacArthur Boulevard in the 1940s to honor General Douglas MacArthur.

Trestle Glen
Near Park Boulevard Way and Grosvenor Place, the site of the trestle that gave the neighborhood its name.

In 1893, Francis Marion "Borax" Smith's Oakland Traction Company built the trestle into the popular resort in Indian Gulch. Mark Twain is said to have taken a ride. The trestle was torn down about 1904.

49

Chinatown District
Webster and 7th streets
Though it is still called Chinatown, Cantonese, Mandarin, Vietnam-ese, Tagalog, Japanese and English are some of the many languages heard on the streets of this area. Street signs and businesses are indentified with Asian characters as well as English text.

Dimond District today
From Prospect Hill. Looking west on MacArthur Boulevard at Lincoln Avenue.

Dimond District
The district was named for Hugh Dimond, who made his home in today's Dimond Park. The Altenheim's 1893 building is visible in the distance on the left.

50

East 14th and High streets today.

Bentley Ostrich Farm
At East 14th and High streets.
Victorian-era hats, fans and feather boas guaranteed a heavy demand for the birds' feathers. The farm was open to visitors year-round for an admission price of 10 cents.

Lake Shore Avenue flood
Three streams run into a culvert under Lake Shore Avenue. Heavy rains caused flooding in the 1930s.

Rainy morning on Lake Shore Avenue in November 2002.

Flood October 13, 1962.
Heavy rains continued to cause flooding in the 1960s.

51

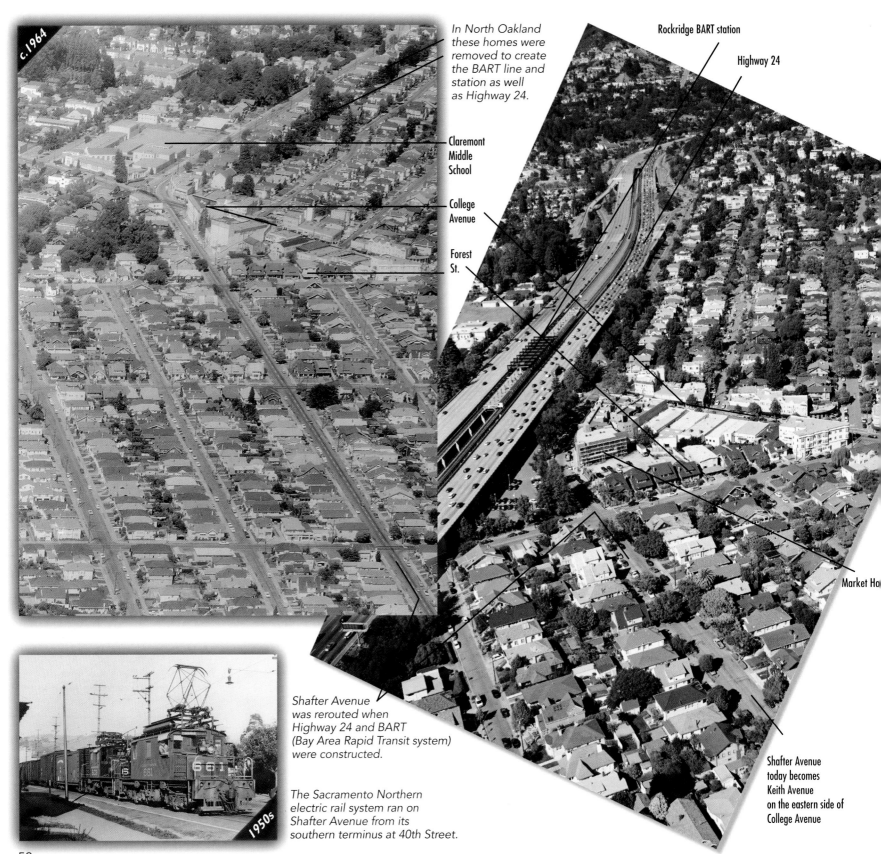

c.1964

In North Oakland these homes were removed to create the BART line and station as well as Highway 24.

Claremont Middle School

College Avenue

Forest St.

Rockridge BART station

Highway 24

Market Ha

Shafter Avenue was rerouted when Highway 24 and BART (Bay Area Rapid Transit system) were constructed.

The Sacramento Northern electric rail system ran on Shafter Avenue from its southern terminus at 40th Street.

Shafter Avenue today becomes Keith Avenue on the eastern side of College Avenue

1950s

661

c.1935

Rockridge Market Hall 5655 College Avenue
Opened in 1986, in approximately the same location as the Free Market.
The Market Hall today houses many individual food shops: produce, fish, meat, prepared food, cheese, bakery, coffee & tea shop, and a restaurant.

◄ **Free Market** 5637-9 College Avenue
Opened in 1918, the Free Market housed a food market with individual shops that included a creamery, produce and fish markets, a bakery, butcher, and a coffee shop.

c.1935

At the Rockridge BART station
On the corner of College and Miles avenues; BART and Highway 24 occupy the former site of the 1935 Bank of America.

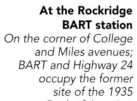

Bank of America
On the corner of College and Shafter avenues. Shafter Avenue was rerouted to create the BART parking lot.

53

2820 Telegraph Avenue
Jack London lived and wrote in this house in 1904.
That location today is between a mortuary and a KFC at Telegraph Avenue and 28th Street.

Residence of Curtis Forrest and family
The house on Webster Street stood across from
the First Presbyterian Church on Broadway.
Mr. Forrest was listed as a capitalist in the Oakland City Directory of 1882.

27th Street
Looking west from Broadway.
The Forrest family residence would have sat
in the middle of 27th Street.

**Family home of
A. K. P. Harmon**
*Mr. Harmon was president
of a silver mine.
Its Webster Street address was
between 21st and 22nd streets.
This huge estate had a
conservatory (on the right)
in the back of the house.
The Harmon Gymnasium on the
UC Berkeley Campus is named for
the Harmon family.*

Today
*Office buildings
stand on the site
where the Harmon
estate was located.*

**◄ Everson family
residence in West Oakland**
*Mr. Everson was an insurance agent.
The house was on the corner of 16th
and Filbert streets. It was destroyed
after the death of Mrs. Everson Sr.*

▲ Kellogg family
*in front of their home at
15th and Grove streets.*

Bud's Body Shop
(Auto Body Repair & Painting)
*1900 Martin Luther King Jr. Way
(formerly Grove St.) at 19th Street.*

**Family residence
of William Moller, Esq.**
*Northeast corner of
Grove and 19th streets.*

20th Street and Broadway
*In the background on the left
is the Kaiser Center near Lake Merritt.*

J. M. Brock family residence
*The house stood at 20th Street and Broadway.
According to the 1886 Oakland City Directory
Mr. Brock was a hardware merchant.
In the background on the left is the bell tower of the
Convent of the Sacred Heart School near Lake Merritt.*

St. Mary's College
*On Broadway between
30th Street and Hawthorne Avenue.
Affectionately known as the "Old Brickpile,"
the school relocated to Moraga in 1928.*

Oakland Auto Row
*Broadway between 30th Street and Hawthorne Ave.
A plaque at 3033 Broadway commemorates
St. Mary's College.*

Brooklyn Presbyterian Church
1144 East 15th Street
Congregation was founded in 1861, the church opened at this location in 1887. Today it is a designated City Landmark.

Synagogue of the First Hebrew Congregation ▶
Originally built at 13th and Clay streets in 1886. The building was moved by the congregation in 1896 to 12th and Castro streets.

Temple Sinai
On 28th Street between Webster Street and Broadway. The congregation moved here in 1914.

First Baptist Church of Oakland
At Telegraph Avenue and 21st Street.
Original congregation was organized in 1854.

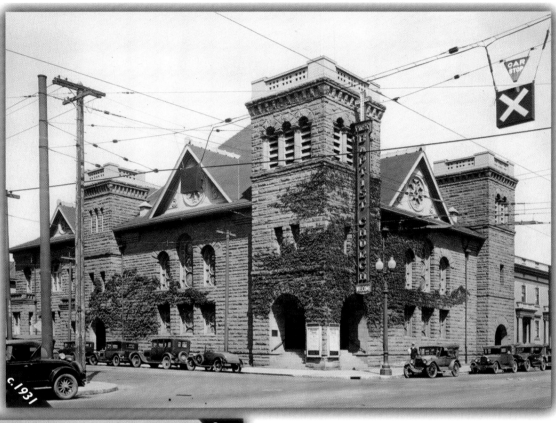

c. 1931

c. 1906

**St. Elizabeth's
Church and Monastery**
*On 34th Avenue above East 14th Street
(today known as International Boulevard).
The church was founded in 1892, built
to serve the German Catholic community.*

**St. Elizabeth's
Church**
*Today's
St. Elizabeth's,
in the same
location, was built
in 1920.
It is an extremely
important part
of the Fruitvale
Hispanic
community.*

59

Moving the Robinson house to Preservation Park
This Queen Anne cottage built in 1891 was originally located on Dimond Avenue in Fruitvale. Of all the homes in Preservation Park, this home made the longest journey to its present site. On the right, Preservation Park under construction. In the foreground, the Robinson house awaits its final placement.

Preservation Park completed in 1991
The houses in Preservation Park represent a unique time in Bay Area architecture, from the Italianate to Queen Anne, Shingle and Craftsman styles.

Robinson house, now restored in Preservation Park
Preservation Park is a unique gathering of small businesses and non-profit organizations that further cultural, social and environmental objectives. Preservation Park is designated as an Historic Preservation District.

Oakland Technical High School

Located at 4351 Broadway in North Oakland. Opened in 1915. City Landmark. It was nominated for City Landmark status by the students in the 1985 senior American Government class.

Merchants Parking garage

This garage sits on the site of the former College of California. There is a commemorative plaque on the garage at the corner of Franklin and 13th streets.

College of California

Henry Durant started a school in 1853. His vision grew to become the College of California. The school was located between 12th and 14th streets from Franklin to Harrison streets. In 1868 the college merged its curriculum with the concept of a State University system. The University of California was founded and moved to the rural community of Berkeley.

Dunsmuir Historic Estate
2960 Peralta Oaks Court
Built in 1899, the house exemplifies Neo-Classical architecture.
Today this 40-acre estate with historic landscaping is designated a
City Landmark and is on the National Register of Historic Places.
Open to the public for tours.

Cohen-Bray House
1440 29th Avenue
Built in 1884,
it contains original
funishings and wallpaper.
Open to the public
on the last Sunday
of each month.
Designated a City
Landmark and on the
National Register of
Historic Places.

c.1875

Residence of the Pardee Family
*The home at 672 11th Street was built by
Enoch Pardee in 1869. Enoch was mayor of Oakland.
His son, George, was also an Oakland mayor and
governor of California from 1902 to 1906.*

Pardee Home Museum
*The home is listed in the National Register of
Historic Places. It is also a California State
Historic Landmark and an Oakland City Landmark.
Open to the public for tours.*

c.1916

Camron-Stanford House
*Built in 1876, the house was just one of many estates on the
shores of Lake Merritt. It is the sole Victorian-era mansion
remaining on Lake Merritt. From 1910 to 1967 it housed the
Oakland Public Museum. A City Landmark, the house is a
also on the National Register of Historic Places;
open for tours and events.*

Alameda County Courthouse
Broadway and 5th Street; served as courthouse from 1874 to 1937, demolished in the 1950s.

**Present
Alameda County Courthouse**
Located at 1225 Fallon near Lake Merritt; opened in 1937.

**Southwest Corner of
14th and Grove streets**
*A vacant lot with billboards.
The First Unitarian Church in the background.*

Oakland Free Library
14th and Grove streets. Dedicated in 1901, the building served as Oakland's main library from 1902 to 1951. Also known as the Charles Greene Library. Remained in operation until 1971.

African-American Museum and Library at Oakland
14th Street at Martin Luther King Jr. Way. Its mission is to discover, preserve, interpret and share the historical and cultural experiences of African-Americans in Northern California. Opened in 2002. City Landmark and on the National Register of Historic Places.

Oakland Tribune Tower

One of the best-known structures on the Oakland skyline. A designated City Landmark. The Oakland Tribune began publication in 1874. The 21-story Tribune Tower was designed by local architect Edward R. Foulkes in Renaissance/Baroque style with Spanish colonial influences.

Fire on Franklin Street in 1950s.

Fire at 371 13th St. Will Rogers Hotel, February 4, 2002

Number 4 Truck
Housed at Station 15 at 427 25th Street.

Number 1 Truck
From Station 1 - 1603 Martin Luther King Jr. Way

Fire Station 13
33rd Avenue and East 12th Street
13 Engine

New rigs Seagrave "White Wagons"
12 and 19 Engines

Fire Station 22
34th and Magnolia streets
Lt. Royal Towns and crew

- In 1853 three fire companies were organized: the Empire, the Washington and the Oakland Hook and Ladder.
- A professional Oakland Fire Department was established in 1869 with a 50-man department.
- The 2002 Oakland Fire Department has 26 stations with a staff of 582.

STATION 19, B SHIFT, 5776 MILES AVENUE, NORTH OAKLAND

| Firefighter Paramedic Michael Schorr 1 year | Firefighter Paramedic Damon Covington 1 year | Firefighter Jeannie Andrews 4 years | Lieutenant Preston Pleasants 10 years | Firefighter Michael Donner 19 years | Engineer Perry Washington 6 years | Captain David Hector 10 years | Firefighter Ed Llamas 12 years |

Oakland Police Department Inspectors

Oakland Police Department Homicide Investigators
top row left to right: .... M. Dunakin, B. Brock;
2nd row from top left to right: .... T. Nolan, P. Green, G. Gallindo;
2nd row from bottom left to r.: .... J. Ferguson, D. Longmire, Lt. B. Theim
bottom row left to right: .... B. Medeiros, L. Cruz, J. Rullamas

Oakland Police Rifle Team was famed for marksmanship
John M. Cockerton, Charles F. Clark, Walter J. Petersen, D.W. Swain, Nick
Williams, H.L. Gilbert, H. B. Gilbert, H.B. Henderson, Ferdinand Schroeder,
H.C. Arnst, L.E. Andrews and Ferdinand Stahle.

Oakland Police Department
Tactical Operations Team

Patrol vehicle of the Oakland Police Department
Driver is Cleland Wells, on the right is Hall B. Rand.
Paddy-wagon at 15th Street near San Pablo Avenue.
Behind the wagon is the police barn and jail.

Patrol vehicles of the Oakland Police Department
Officer Burke, Officer Dean, Sergeant Van Sloten.

Oakland's first traffic unit – created in 1914
From left: Les Manning, Henry Avila, A. Morgenthal, Anthony Lillenthal.
Charles Hemphill on extreme right was in charge of the four-man squad.

Oakland Police Department Traffic Division
From left to right: Jamie Kim, Sam Faleafine, Chris Moreno,
Randy Pope, Rich Williams, Mike Randall

Horace Carpentier,
Mayor 1854-1855

Elected the first mayor of Oakland. He was reviled as the man who tied up Oakland's waterfront for personal gain for the last half of the nineteenth century.

George C. Pardee,
Mayor 1893-1895

He was the first native son of California to serve as Oakland mayor, as well as the first California governor born in the state.

John L. Davie,
Mayor 1895-97 and 1915-31

Served longer as mayor than any other individual. During his tenure industry expanded, the harbor was developed and the airport was constructed.

Frank K. Mott,
Mayor 1905-1915

Known for regaining the rights to the waterfront, as well as for creating many public works projects, including new improvements of sewers, streets, electricity, fire and police protection, also for building the current city hall and establishing the Oakland Public Museum.

Lionel Wilson,
Mayor 1977-1990

Grew up in Oakland, graduated from McClymonds High School, UC Berkeley and Hastings College of Law. Practiced law in Oakland until 1960 when he was appointed to the Oakland-Piedmont Municipal Court as Alameda County's first black judge. He was the first African-American Mayor of Oakland, who opened job opportunities for blacks in corporate and city government.

Edmund G. (Jerry) Brown Jr.,
Mayor 1999-present

Served as California governor from 1974 until 1982. His central focus as Mayor has been to revitalize the city and bring development downtown in a spirit of "elegant density". In his first term more than 350 companies opened and 10,000 jobs were created and property values increased by $4 billion.

Oakland City Government 2001 – 2002

*Top row left to right: Danny Wan – District 2; Roland Smith – City Auditor; Henry Chang – Councilmember at Large; Nancy Nadel – District 3;
Robert Bobb – City Manager; John Russo – City Attorney; Larry Reid – Vice Mayor. Seated left to right: Richard Spees – District 4;
Ceda Floyd – City Clerk; Edmund G. Brown Jr. – Mayor; Jane Brunner – District 1; Ignacio de la Fuente – District 5, City Council President.*

Memorial for victims of the September 11th attacks, September 14, 2001
City officials and Oaklanders were in attendance in Frank H. Ogawa Plaza.

Railroad Station
On 7th Street between Washington Street and Broadway

Oakland's First Railway Station
Local train service began September 2, 1863 with engineer James Batchelder at the throttle of Liberty, pulling three "handmade" cars to the ferry landing at the foot of Seventh Street. This station served as a downtown stop for transcontinental railroad passengers.

Central Pacific Railroad Station
On the pediment, the monogram CPRR stands for the Central Pacific Railroad, below it the S. P. stands for Southern Pacific. The line operated as the Central Pacific until the Southern Pacific Railroad Company took over in 1885. The station was built in 1874, closed in 1941.

Legal Assistance for Seniors
Occupies the building today. The original 1874 station has been remodeled but is still recognizable. The Mi Rancho grocery and tortilla factory was located here until 1996. A designated City Landmark.

Freight Train on the Embarcadero
Numerous freight and passenger trains travel on the Embarcadero as they pass through Oakland.

C. L. Dellums Amtrak Station
C. L. Dellums served as president and vice president of the Brotherhood of Sleeping Car Porters, the first African-American trade union in American history. Opened in 1995.

Oakland Airport

According to Woody Minor in "Pacific Gateway", transoceanic flights of 1927 brought instant fame to Oakland's fledgling airport. Charles Lindbergh dedicated the field, which then consisted of one long runway and little else.

Many historic flights embarked from Oakland, including the first flights to Hawaii. Within two years, a modern and sophisticated facility would take shape on the Bay Farm Island marsh.

Prior to World War II, Oakland ranked as Northern California's leading commercial airport. After World War II the Oakland Municipal Airport would gain new prominence as the headquarters for a succession of charter airlines. It remains one of the nation's most historic aviation sites.

The original Oakland Airport, known today as "North Field"

Oakland International Airport terminal

Oakland International Airport

Passenger volumes at Oakland have tripled since the early 1980s. Much of this traffic has been generated by high-volume, short-haul carriers like Southwest flying up and down the coast. In 1998, the airport's twenty-gates handled 9.2 million passengers. In 2002, domestic scheduled service was offered by nine airlines; Alaska, Aloha, American, America West, Continental, Delta, Jet Blue, Southwest and United. International scheduled: Allegro, Mexicana Scheduled Charter: North American and Ryan International (SunTrips) and Regional: American Eagle, Skywest, Mesa.

Picnickers on Yerba Buena Island

Seen in the distance, the Long Wharf – the wharf on the left – was used for shipping, while the Oakland Mole on the right was used for passengers.

Inside the Oakland Mole

The Oakland Mole with trains and passengers.

The Key Route Pier as viewed from San Francisco Bay

The Bay Bridge under construction

The Key Route Pier continued to serve while the bridge was being built.

Yerba Buena Island with the Key Route Pier

The pier, on the left, extended over 3 miles into the Bay. It served commuters traveling to and from San Francisco and the East Bay.

This photograph was taken prior to the construction of Treasure Island, which was built to house the 1939 World's Fair.

The Key Route Pier
Bay Bridge construction is getting underway with the Key Route Pier on the right. The Bay Bridge was completed in 1936.

Bay Bridge and Yerba Buena Island
Looking east toward Berkeley, Emeryville and Oakland.

AC Transit buses
A line of buses at the corner of College and Shafter avenues near the Rockridge BART station waits to load passengers en route to a University of California Golden Bears football game.

Horse Railway *A car of the Broadway & Piedmont Horse Railway. This five-foot-gauge railway was organized in 1876. The line began at Seventh and Washington streets, and took passengers six miles round-trip along Broadway to Piedmont Avenue and Mountain View Cemetery. According to the infomation on the back of this photo, the boy standing at the side of the car is Henry Nedderman, Oakland's future chief of police.*

BART (Bay Area Rapid Transit) train
Entering MacArthur station.
Since 1972, passengers have traveled more than 22 billion miles on the system. BART has a 103-mile system with 43 stations.

Steam Train on Telegraph Avenue at 51st Street
Trains replaced exhausted horses at 40th Street en route to Berkeley. Electric streetcars later replaced the horsecars and steam trains. The first building on the left still stands today; a City Landmark, it houses G & G Hardware and Plumbing.

Quiet street at the turn of 20th Century
This bucolic stretch of Peralta Avenue ran along Peralta Creek.
The street was renamed Coolidge Avenue when Fruit Vale (now the
Fruitvale district) was incorporated into the city of Oakland in 1909.
The city already had a Peralta Street in West Oakland.

Dawn of 21st Century - The MacArthur Maze
Interstates 880 and 980 and Highway 24 converge; BART trains run below.

Key Route Piedmont Avenue Station
Station was located between 40th and 41th streets on Piedmont Avenue.
This was the end of the line for the Key Route's C-line. The electric trains traveled
on the Key Route Pier to the bay where passengers boarded a ferry to San Francisco.

41st Street and Piedmont Avenue
A plaque dedicated to the Key Route System stands
on the little plaza to the right of the clock tower.

c.1881

Alameda/Oakland Ferry – the Peralta

Ferryboat Oakland

The ferryboat Oakland began life as the steamboat Chrysopolis. In 1875 the Central Pacific Railroad purchased and refurbished her as double-end ferry. She served in that capacity and carried more passengers through the Estuary and across to San Francisco than any other ferryboat. She was rebuilt in 1898 and again in 1920. Early in 1940, while lying at the southern Alameda shore, her hull caught fire and she was destroyed.

c.1870

c.1972

On the Oakland Pier

The first Pullman train arrives from Boston on the Oakland Pier, which extended 6,900 feet into the bay from 7th Street.

BART (Bay Area Rapid Transit)

A train in the trans-bay tube on the bottom of the bay. The BART system opened in 1972. Since beginning operations, BART has carried nearly 2 billion passengers.

c.1938

**East 12th Avenue
at 22nd Street**

Paramount Theatre
2025 Broadway
Paramount Pictures opened this movie palace in 1931. This 3,000-seat auditorium is Oakland's premier venue for entertainment and events. It has City, State and National Historic Landmark status. Official theater of the Oakland Ballet and the Oakland East Bay Symphony.

Parkway Theater
At 1834 Park Boulevard, opened in 1925. Today it presents movies in an innovative "Picture, Pub and Pizza" setting.

Grand Lake Theater
3200 Grand Avenue. Opened in 1926 with Irma Falvey at the Mighty Wurlitzer.
This exquisitely maintained theatre is a designated City Landmark and a mainstay of the Grand Lake commercial district.
The Mighty Wurlitzer organ is still played on Friday and Saturday evenings.

Fox Oakland Theater

The theater opened on Telegraph Avenue October 26, 1928. A luxury movie palace. Theatergoers could also enjoy vaudeville performances.

Lighting of restored marquee in November 2001. A designated City Landmark, also on the National Register of Historic Places, the Oakland Fox is awaiting new life.

Oakland Ballet

*Performance of "Rite of Spring" in 1976
at the Paramount Theatre.*

*Performance of "Jinx" in 2002
at the Paramount Theatre.*

**The original Oakland Symphony
with Gerhard Samuel conducting**

**Oakland East Bay Symphony and Chorus
with Michael Morgan conducting**
Performances at the Paramount Theatre.

Childrens' Fairyland under construction
Opened in 1950, Childrens' Fairyland was the first storybook theme park in the nation. Visitors passed through the classic "old woman in the shoe" set in order to enter a fantasy world of magic and imagination.

The Shoe
For the millions of children from all around the world who have visited Children's Fairyland over the years, "the shoe" remains the symbol of welcome and the invitation to enjoy a day of family fun.

Puppeteers at the first Fairyland Puppet Fair
The Storybook Puppet Theater at Children's Fairyland was opened in 1956. The puppeteers are posing before a performance of Sleeping Beauty. Pictured left to right: Noel, Mary McMahon, Patricia Lavin and Lewis Mahlmann.

The Storybook Puppet Theatre puppeteers today
The internationally renowned puppet theater has inspired many young people to enter the profession, including Frank Oz (Miss Piggy and Yoda) who apprenticed at the theater in the 1960s. Pictured left to right: Randal Metz, Roxanne Burk, Jacqueline Lynaugh and Lewis Mahlmann. Lewis Mahlmann has served as the theater's director for 35 years.

Chabot Observatory

Anthony Chabot, a successful hydraulic engineer, provided water to the city of Oakland. Chabot funded an 8-inch telescope and the new observatory, which opened in Lafayette Square, downtown Oakland on November 24th, 1883.

Lafayette Square today

The urban park between 10th and 11th streets and Jefferson Street and Martin Luther King Jr. Way, is designated a City Landmark. The mound in the recently redesigned park commemorates the Observatory.

Chabot Space and Science Center
Located in the Oakland hills at 10000 Skyline Boulevard.

Chabot Space and Science Center

The state-of-the-art science center features the observatory domes on the left, Tien MegaDome Theater in the foreground and the Ask Jeeves Planetarium on the right. Offering hands-on interactive science and technology exhibits, teacher training, student labs and public science programs. Free telescope viewing is offered on Friday and Saturday evenings, per Anthony Chabot's stipulation. It opened in August 2000.

Elephants at the Oakland Zoo
*The Oakland Zoo in Knowland Park opened in 1936.
Located at 9777 Golf Links Road, the Zoo is open 363 days a year
and has extensive educational programs.*

African Elephant Exhibit today
*Opened in 1989. The Zoo today has over
400 native and exotic animals from around the world
represented by 100 different species in 58 exhibits.*

Primate Exhibit
*The remarkable difference between the past and present animal habitats at the Zoo reflects the change
of focus for zoos around the world from circus-like exhibition setting to more educational and
more sensitive to the well-being of the animals. On the right is "Gibbon Island" which opened in 1990.*

85

Fabiola Hospital
Located on Moss Avenue (now MacArthur Boulevard) and Howe Street.
One of Oakland's first hospitals. Originally founded as the
Oakland Homeopathic Hospital and Dispensary.

Kaiser Permanente Hospital
Located on MacArthur Boulevard at Howe Steet.
Kaiser Permanente is the oldest and among the largest
integrated health care delivery systems in the nation.

Piedmont Baths
Located near 27th and Harrison streets. Piedmont Baths offered a tank filled
with pure salt water (70 by 120 feet), a diving platform 45 feet high, and an
assortment of other recreational activities. The building on the far left was the
powerhouse for the Consolidated Piedmont Cable Company, whose
operations heated the water for the baths.

Today a vacant lot
Located at Bay Place and 27th and Harrison streets.
The powerhouse was remodeled into an auto showroom in 1925,
and housed the Cox Cadillac dealership for many years.
The building is now boarded-up and awaiting restoration.

Sequoyah Country Club
11th Hole
Sequoyah Country Club was founded in 1913.

Sequoyah Country Club
11th Hole – known as "The Burn"
Sequoyah has earned the title among golfers as the best kept secret in the Bay Area. The 11th hole is a long 453 yards with a tricky large green, which makes many feel "The Burn" – the most difficult hole on the course.

Lawn Bowling in Lakeside Park
Green Number One was opened for play on June 15, 1912.
Pictured from left to right; unidentified, N. Deir, J. Taylor, unidentified, the boy is Alex Bowen, J. Smith, unidentified.

Oakland Lawn Bowling Club
The Oakland Lawn Bowling Club offers free lessons to the public. The clubhouse and bowling green are City Landmarks. Pictured from left to right: Norman Lum, John Chinn, Jerry Ridley, Hailey Knott, Jerry Knott, Paul Schmidt.

Cypress Freeway – Aftermath of the Loma Prieta 7.1 Earthquake
Triangle Coffee Shop on the left at 26th and Cypress streets.
October 19th, 1989 two days after the quake.
Forty-two people were killed when the two-tiered Cypress Freeway collapsed.

Thirteen years after
Triangle Coffee Shop on the left at 26th and Cypress streets. The freeway was demolished, the street was renamed Mandela Parkway.

Cypress Freeway – Recovery Procedures
At approximately 10th Street. One month after the earthquake.
Heavy damage from the quake was sustained in West Oakland.

The Mandela Parkway median strip
At approximately 10th Street and Mandela Parkway.
The Cypress Freeway was never rebuilt.

Oakland Hills Fire

Aftermath of the disasterous firestorm that burned for three days starting October 20, 1991. Twenty-five people died, approximately 3,000 structures were destroyed. The fire burned nearly 1,600 acres in the Oakland and Berkeley hills causing well over $1.5 billion in property damage.

New homes built on the site of the fire with the San Francisco Bay in the distance.

Two weeks after the firestorm.
This location is believed to be Golden Gate Avenue.

Fire area after over a decade of new construction.

Oakland Baseball Team
1889 California Champions
Oakland's baseball tradition
goes back to the 1860s.

Oakland Oaks of the
Pacific Coast League
The Oaks won the PCL Championship
in 1912, 1927, 1948 and 1950.
In the early days of the PCL,
teams played close
to 200 games a season.

Oakland Larks
The Larks played in the West Coast Negro Baseball
League in 1946. They won the championship of the
W.C.N.B.L. with 36 wins and only 12 losses. The Larks
continued on the barnstorming circuit, playing ex-
hibition games in the west and mid-west until 1949.
Lionel "Lefty" Wilson was an ace pitcher for the
Larks, he went on to serve as mayor of Oakland from
1977 to 1990.
Pictured left to right: unidentified player, Milton Pool,
Johnny Allen, unidentified player.

**Oakland Athletics
1972, 1973, 1974
World Series
Champions**

**2002
Oakland Athletics**
*Western Division
Champions
103 wins 59 losses.*

*Miguel Tejada
was honored as the
American League Most
Valuable Player.*

*Barry Zito
received the
American League
Cy Young award.*

1974 - 1975 Golden State Warriors

The 1974-75 Golden State Warriors won the NBA Championship, the franchise's only title since moving to the West Coast in 1962.
The team was led by NBA Finals MVP Rick Barry (#24) and NBA Rookie of the Year Keith Wilkes (#41).
Alvin Attles (seated fourth from the left on the bottom row) was the team's Head Coach.

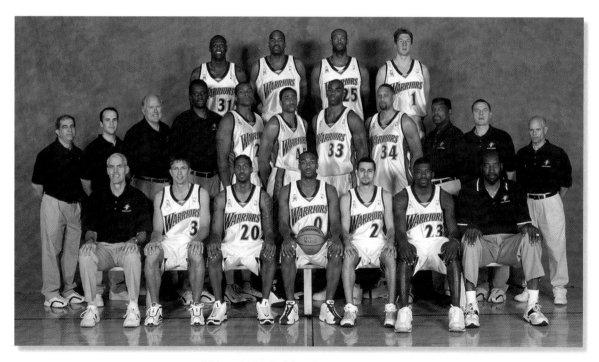

2001 - 2002 Golden State Warriors

Bridging the past and the present, Warriors Vice President and Assistant General Manager Al Attles (third from the right in the middle row)
has spent 43 years with the Warriors as either a player, coach or front office executive. Antawn Jamison (#33) was the team's leading scorer,
while Jason Richardson (#23) won the NBA Slam Dunk Contest during his rookie season.

American Football League Oakland Raiders 1963

First year head coach and general manager Al Davis (top row, left) led the Raiders to a record of 10 wins and 4 losses.
(In 1962 the Raiders were 1-13).

National Football League Oakland Raiders 2002

AFC Champions, Western Division Champions for the third year in a row. Rich Gannon (#12) named MVP player of the NFL.

Sources

Oakland, The Story of a City:
by Beth Bagwell
Presidio Press, 1982
reprinted by Oakland Heritage Alliance, 1994

The Spirit of Oakland: An Anthology
Heritage Media Corp., 2000
Carlsbad, California

The Peraltas and Their Houses,
Alameda County Historical Society, 1998

The Beginnings of Oakland California, A.U.C.
By Peter Thomas Conmy, City Librarian
Oakland Public Library, 1961

Pacific Gateway,
An Illustrated History of the Port of Oakland
Woodruff Minor
Communications Division, Port of Oakland, 2002

The Pacific Coast League, 1903-1988
by Bill O'Neal

Contemporary Biography of California's
Representative Men, Vol. 2
A.L. Bancroft and Co. Publishers, 1882

Photography Credits

1 — 1854 Illustrated post card - private collection of Steve Costa
1 — 2002 Aerial Photograph Bill Caldwell
8 — 1879 Panoramic Photograph Behrman, courtesy Oakland History Room, Oakland Public Library
8 — 2002 Panoramic Photograph Bill Caldwell
12 — Document and 1952 Photographs courtesy Oakland History Room, Oakland Public Library
13 — 2002 Photographs by Bill Caldwell
16 — 1806 painting by G. H. von Langsdorff titled Dance of the Indians in the Mission San Jose
       in New California, courtesy Bancroft Archives
16 — 1806 painting by G. H. von Langsdorff, Natives fishing, courtesy Bancroft Archives
16 — 2002 Photographers Bill Caldwell, Hasain Rasheed
17 — Illustration of Vicente Peralta by Ernest Narjoi
17 — llustrations of Peralta homes by Robert Gilliland
17 — 2002 Photographers Bill Caldwell, Hasain Rasheed
17 — Plaque design by Jeff Norman
18 — Map plotted by Julius Kellersberger, courtesy Oakland History Room, Oakland Public Library
19 — 1998 map, City of Oakland, Community and Economic Development Agency
19 — 2002 redesigned for this publication by Milan Hájek
20 — 2002 Photograph by Bill Caldwell
20 — circa 1869 Photograph courtesy Oakland History Room, Oakland Public Library
20 — 2002 Photograph by Bill Caldwell
20 — circa 1873 Photograph courtesy Oakland History Room, Oakland Public Library
21 — 2002 Photograph by Bill Caldwell
21 — circa 1894 Illustration, from the book G.A.R. 27th Annual Encampment Views of Oakland,
         California, Pacific Press Publishing Company
21 — 2002 Photograph by Bill Caldwell
21 — circa 1874 Photograph courtesy Oakland History Room, Oakland Public Library
22 — 1896 The Illustrated Directory of Oakland, courtesy Oakland History Room, Oakland Public Library
22 — 2002 Photograph by Bill Caldwell
23 — 1896 The Illustrated Directory of Oakland, courtesy Oakland History Room, Oakland Public Library
       2002 Photograph by Bill Caldwell
24 — circa 1935 Photograph courtesy Oakland History Room, Oakland Public Library
24 — circa 1932 Photograph courtesy Oakland History Room, Oakland Public Library
24 — 2002 Illustrations by Milan Hájek
24 — 2002 Photograph by Bill Caldwell
25 — 1896 The Illustrated Directory of Oakland, courtesy Oakland History Room, Oakland Public Library
25 — 2002 Photograph by Bill Caldwell
26 — circa 1854 Photograph courtesy Oakland History Room, Oakland Public Library
26 — circa 1869 Photograph courtesy Oakland History Room, Oakland Public Library
26 — circa 1876 Photograph courtesy Oakland History Room, Oakland Public Library
26 — circa 1914 Photograph courtesy Oakland History Room, Oakland Public Library
27 — 1961 Photograph courtesy Oakland History Room, Oakland Public Library
27 — 2002 Photograph by Bill Caldwell
27 — 1954 Photograph courtesy Oakland History Room, Oakland Public Library
27 — 2002 Photograph by Bill Caldwell
28 — 1869 Photograph courtesy Oakland History Room, Oakland Public Library
28 — circa 1900 Photograph courtesy Oakland History Room, Oakland Public Library
29 — circa 1912 Photograph courtesy Oakland History Room, Oakland Public Library
29 — 2002 Photograph by Bill Caldwell
30 — circa 1930 Photograph courtesy Oakland History Room, Oakland Public Library
30 — 1964 Photograph courtesy Oakland History Room, Oakland Public Library
31 — 2002 Photographs by Bill Caldwell
32 — circa 1879 Photograph courtesy Oakland History Room, Oakland Public Library
32 — 2002 Photograph by Bill Caldwell
32 — 1871 Illustration courtesy Oakland History Room, Oakland Public Library

Books About Oakland

Oakland, the Story of a City,
Beth Bagwell
(Novato: Presidio Press, 1982).
Still the warmest and most poetic telling of the Oakland story.
Bagwell was the first president of the
Oakland Heritage Alliance.

The Second Gold Rush:
Oakland and the East Bay During World War II,
Marilynn S. Johnson
(Berkeley: University of California Press, 1993)
A social and political history of Oakland and the East Bay as it
was transformed by wartime industry and the influx of domes-
tic migrants

Pacific Gateway:
An Illustrated History of the Port of Oakland,
Woodruff Minor
(Oakland: Port of Oakland, 2000).
Excellent photos, maps, and documentation of Oakland's Port
and Airport. Produced as an impact-mitigation measure for
the demolition of the Grove Street Pier transit shed.

The Spirit of Oakland: An Anthology,
Abby Wasserman and Diane Curry
(Carlsbad, CA: Heritage Media: 2000).
The latest entry, with essays by numerous local authors; pays
particular attention to individual neighborhoods.

Oakland, Hub of the West,
David Weber
(Tulsa, OK,Continental Heritage Press, 1981)
Oakland's history from its earliest days to 1980 with many
vintage photos from the Oakland Museum.

Through These Doors:
Discovering Oakland at Preservation Park,
Helaine Kaplan Prentice, Betty Marvin,
Andrew Brubaker, Terry Lim
(Oakland, Preservation Park, 1996)
A lavishly illustrated book on Oakland's history as told through
the stories of the homes and owners in Preservation Park.

For a more extensive list visit the Oakland History Room at the
Oakland Public Library Main Branch at 125–14th Street.
Oakland History Room – 510-238-3222

Also visit www.oaklandhistory.com click on Book List

Oakland Tours Programs

City Tours - 510-238-3234
Mountain View Cemetery - 510-772-5209
Oakland Heritage Alliance - 510-763-9218

Websites

For descriptions of Attractions in Oakland:
Dining and Entertainment, Sports and Recreation, Shopping,
Tours, Itineraries and Business Services.

www.oaklandnet.com (City of Oakland's website)

www.oaklandcvb.com (Oakland Convention and Visitors Bureau)

www.oaklandhistory.com (Oakland vintage photographs)

www.oaklandphotojourney.com (The digital version of this book)

www.chabotspace.org (Chabot Space and Science Center)

www.fairyland.org (Children's Fairyland)

www.gondolaservizio.com (Gondola Servizio)

www.woodminster.com (Joaquin Miller Park/Woodminster Amphitheater)

www.oaklandice.com (Oakland Ice Center)

www.oaklandzoo.org (Oakland Zoo)

www.portofoakland.com (Port of Oakland)

www.dunsmuir.org (Dunsmuir House & Gardens Historic Estate)

www.paramounttheatre.com (Paramount Theatre)

www.pardeehome.org (Pardee Home Museum)

www.preservationpark.com (Preservation Park)

www.USSPotomac.org (USS Potomac)

www.mills.edu (Mills College Art Museum)

www.mocha.org (The Museum of Children's Art)

www.museumca.org (Oakland Museum of California)

www.aerospace.org – (Western Aerospace Museum)

www.asianculture.org – (Oakland Asian Cultural Center)

www.oaklandballet.org – (Oakland Ballet)

www.oebs.org – (Oakland East Bay Symphony)

www.oyo.org – (Oakland Youth Orchestra)

www.oaklandheritage.org - (Oakland Heritage Alliance)

www.weloveoakland.com - (We love Oakland)

www.nonchalance.org

jacklondongeo@hotmail.com, Jack London Club 510-436-6868

Bill Caldwell, photographer, owner and creative director of Momentum Publications

Photographer – for over 25 years. Specializing in large format panoramic images, creating extremely large California panoramic prints.
Clients include: The Oakland Athletics, Pacific Bell Directory, San Francisco Newspaper Agency, Save the Bay (non-profit organization located in Oakland), the Red and White Fleet, Holiday Inn in San Francisco. Images have been used for postcards, posters, advertisements, fine art and mural prints.

Momentum Publications – Publisher of the Photo Directory since 1996 and the Oakland - A photographic journey. The directory serves Northern California creative professionals: photographers, art directors, art buyers and graphic designers The Photo Directory is a resource guide containing all things photographic and digital imaging in Northern California. Over 20,000 creative professionals depend on the Photo Directory. www.PhotoDirectory.ws is the Web site version of the printed directory, receiving over a million hits since the summer of 2000. Oakland - A photographic journey is the first of two photography books about Oakland.

Creative Team

Dennis Evanosky, writer, historian

Dennis Evanosky is the special sections editor at Hills Newspapers, where he has combined newspaper work with his love of Oakland history. In 1997, with Hills Newspapers' sponsorship, he helped create an Oakland Heritage Alliance award-winning calendar that celebrated his Oakland neighborhood, the Laurel district. Since then, he and his partner, Eric Kos, have created four more calendars featuring Oakland's city halls, rail and streetcar transportation, the estuary and most recently the Civil War and Mountain View Cemetery, where he serves as a docent.
Visit his website www.Oaklandhistory.com.

Hasain Rasheed, photographer

Hasain Rasheed, an Oakland native, is one of the young talented photographers of his generation. His portfolio includes a variety of sports, portraits and photo journalistic images that gives the viewer an instant sense of time and spontaneity. Hasain's photographs have been published in The Oakland Tribune, Urb Magazine and various print and internet publications. Hasain is a self-taught photographer who holds a degree in Animation and Digital Video.

Milan Hájek, graphic designer

Native of Czech Republic, Milan studied urban planning & computer science at Prague Technical University. He fled the communist oppression in the mid 80s, headed for California and started out in the printing industry in Oakland as a graphic designer. He credits plenty of classical art education and art exposure for his "natural sense of harmony and equilibrium". In 1991 he started his own firm, GRADEENT DESIGN. He has won several awards for print design from PINC (Printing Industries of Northern California).
Visit his website www.gradeent.com